Brilliant Eats

Simple and Delicious Recipes for Anyone Who Wants to Be KidneyWise™

Written by

Kelly L. Welsh, R.D., C.D.
Renal Dietitian
Polycystic Kidney Disease Patient
Wife and Mother

Reviewed by

Poonhar Poon, M.S, R.D., L.D.N.

Janelle E. Gonyea, R.D., L.D.

Anne-Marie Desai, R.D.

Brilliant Eats
Simple and Delicious Recipes for Anyone Who Wants to Be KidneyWise™

www.kidneywise.org

ISBN: 978-0-9816166-0-5

Published by the PKD Foundation
9221 Ward Parkway, Suite 400
Kansas City, MO 64114-3367
www.pkdcure.org

Manufactured by
Favorite Recipes® Press
An imprint of

FRP.

P. O. Box 305142
Nashville, Tennessee 37230
1-800-358-0560

Food Styling by Vicky Johnson
Leawood, KS
913-909-9598

Recipe Photography by Blaine Fisher Commercial Photography
5638 Nall Avenue
Mission, KS 66202
www.blainefisherphotography.com

Designed by Voltage Creative
524 Walnut Street, Suite 220
Kansas City, MO 64106
www.voltagecreative.com

Dedication

More than 41 million Americans are affected by kidney disease. Another 20 million are at risk. Although there is no cure, nutrition is one way to fight the causes of kidney failure, including diabetes, polycystic kidney disease, obesity, and high blood pressure.

The KidneyWise™ Nutrition Program was designed to help patients and loved ones affected by kidney disease—and the many more simply interested in overall kidney health—maintain a happy, healthy, and KidneyWise™ lifestyle.

Brilliant Eats: Simple and Delicious Recipes for Anyone Who Wants to Be KidneyWise™ is one component of the KidneyWise™ Nutrition Program. To learn more, visit www.kidneywise.org.

All proceeds from book sales will benefit the PKD Foundation, the only organization worldwide dedicated to finding a treatment and cure for polycystic kidney disease (PKD). PKD is one of the most common, life-threatening genetic diseases, affecting 12.5 million children and adults around the world. The PKD Foundation fights PKD through research funding and patient education. Headquartered in Kansas City, Missouri, the PKD Foundation operates volunteer-led Chapters in more than 65 cities worldwide. To learn more about PKD and the PKD Foundation, visit www.pkdcure.org or call 1-800-PKD-CURE.

www.kidneywise.org

For Research in
Polycystic Kidney Disease

www.pkdcure.org

Disclaimer: In beginning any new diet plan, it is always important to first consult your physician. Nowhere is this more important than in the case of individuals facing genetic or acquired diseases. Although this book was developed with the kidney disease patient in mind, it is also appropriate for anyone interested in a KidneyWise™ nutrition plan.

The recipes in this book are not intended to cure kidney disease; they are intended to help those affected by kidney disease in meeting the specific needs of their condition at the time of intake. Regular consumption of the meals shared here will not replace you regularly seeing your general physician or nephrologist. By maintaining desired lab values, receiving physician care, and consuming a proper diet, kidney disease patients can often minimize the manifestation of symptoms and postpone the need for dialysis and transplantation.

A Note from the Author

I never dreamed I would have the opportunity to be involved in a project that could help so many people! When first approached by the PKD Foundation, the cookbook started out as a small manual, featuring general diet guidelines and recipes for polycystic kidney disease (PKD) patients. But as we moved farther along in the writing, it became apparent that anyone with kidney disease—or anyone interested in overall kidney nutrition, for that matter—could benefit greatly from these easy, delicious, and nutritious recipes! So our project grew. And so did my excitement.

As a dietitian—and a mom—my philosophy on nutrition is all about being realistic. I refuse to take the individual person and blanket them with a strict, unreasonable, textbook diet plan. Instead, dietary changes will only be successful if they taste good and are fairly easy to follow. This couldn't be more true in my own family, where time is of the essence, and I have to create meals appealing to all ages. So, with this cookbook, I tried to give the reader options, while including familiar favorites and some new ideas.

For my husband (the true chef in the family) and me, some of our favorite recipes include Easy Bruschetta, Roasted Corn and Edamame Salad, Hearts of Palm Salad with Ruby Red Grapefruit and Dungeness Crab, and Grilled Salmon with Papaya-Mint Salsa.

Some of my children's favorite recipes include Noodles Romano, Grilled Asparagus and Mozzarella, Honey Garlic Pork Chops, and Filet with Pesto.

Whatever your favorites, I hope you enjoy the labor of love that's turned into *Brilliant Eats: Simple and Delicious Recipes for Anyone Who Wants to Be KidneyWise™*. It's my hope and strong conviction that this cookbook, above all others, brings the kidney diet back to reality—giving real people and real families tasty options that fall within your kidney dietary needs. Always keep in mind that moderation is key, variety helps, and food should be enjoyable! So from our kitchen to yours . . . bon appétit!

Best wishes,

Kelly L. Welsh. R.D., C.D.

Kelly L. Welsh, R.D., C.D.

4

Table of Contents

Roasted Vegetable Salad, *page 37*

Basic KidneyWise™ Nutrition Guidelines

Healthy kidneys get rid of the wastes that come from food once the body has used all of the nutrition in it. When kidneys no longer work properly, it is often necessary to change the way a person eats to avoid build-up of these wastes.

Nutrients to Know

Although every person needs their own specific diet, there are several nutrients that all renal diets include:

- Calcium and phosphorus
- Sodium
- Fluids
- Potassium
- Protein
- Calories

Learning to read labels and examine recipes, while knowing which foods contain the largest amounts of these nutrients, will help you follow your meal plan. Here is a closer look at these nutrients.

Calcium and phosphorus, in the right balance, work together in the body to keep your teeth and bones strong, and a change in one can cause a change in the other. If the kidneys fail, phosphorus may build up in your blood. Less phosphorus must be eaten for meals and snacks. It is also usually necessary to take a phosphate binder with meals and snacks. This is a medicine used to grab hold of the phosphorus in the food and keep it from getting into the blood. A high phosphorus level in the blood can cause many problems, including itching, bone pain, brittle bones, muscle aches and heart damage.

Sodium is found in the diet most commonly as salt. Limiting salt intake helps control blood pressure and fluid buildup. In addition to the salt shaker, there are other sources of high-sodium foods such as processed meats, including bacon, sausage, and luncheon meats. Snack foods, canned foods, and frozen prepared meals also contain large amounts of salt.

Fluids in the diet are beverages such as water, milk, and juice, as well as foods that melt at room temperature, such as ice cream. Fluids may need to be limited. Watching fluids helps to control blood pressure and puts less strain on the heart, which has to pump that fluid throughout the body.

> **The diet prescribed for kidney disease patients depends on several things:**
> - The stage of kidney failure—early, middle, or late
> - The kind of dialysis chosen
> - Whether or not diabetes is also present
> - Height and weight
> - Activity level
> - Amount of urine output

Potassium is a mineral present in many fruits and vegetables, as well as dairy products. If your kidneys do not work well, potassium can build up in the blood. Too much or too little potassium in the diet can affect the muscles in the body, particularly the heart. Some medications can cause your body to retain or excrete excessive potassium. Dairy products, dried fruits, and legumes are also good sources of potassium but are high in phosphorus and may need to be limited. Salt substitutes containing potassium chloride are also high in potassium and should not be used unless directed by your physician.

Protein is needed daily to build muscles, repair tissues, and fight infection. Protein is the nutrient most needed to prevent malnutrition. Protein is present in many food items, but the highest-quality protein is found in animal proteins, like beef, pork, poultry, seafood, and eggs. Well-nourished patients get sick less often and live longer. It is important to include some protein each and every day.

Calories are needed to supply energy and to maintain weight. Calories come from all the foods you eat, including proteins, carbohydrates, and fat. Calories are a concern if weight is too low or too high. Sometimes special liquid supplements are needed to provide enough calories to maintain weight or regain lost weight.

The kidney-friendly diet can be challenging. On the following pages are recipes to help you no matter where your kidney function is and/or what treatment plan you are currently following.

Always remember:
- Each person's diet should be individualized by a physician and/or dietitian.
- No two people should be following the exact same diet.
- Everyone has different needs based on disease states, lab results, weight loss/gain, protein needs, etc.
- Know your lab results and what they mean. Your lab results are the key to balancing your kidney diet. Also keep in mind that labs may change from month to month. It is extremely important to know what your lab results are and to be able to translate that into what foods, vitamins, and minerals your body needs.

To be considered a KidneyWise™ food, a product must meet all of the following nutritional levels, which are based on a standard serving size as specified by the FDA for an individual food.

A serving of the food product must:
- Be low in potassium (less than 200 milligrams);
- Be low in phosphorus (less than or equal to 100 milligrams);
- Be low in fat (less than or equal to 3 grams);
- Be low in cholesterol (less than or equal to 20 milligrams);
- Be a significant fiber source (contain 3 or more grams of fiber);
- Be low in sodium (less than or equal to 140 milligrams);
- Contain at least 10 percent of the Daily Value of one or more of these naturally occurring nutrients: Vitamin A, Vitamin D, Vitamin C, B- vitamins or Iron; and
- Contain the essential fatty acid Omega 3's.

Grilled Salmon with Papaya-Mint Salsa, *page 59*

Guidelines for the Pre-Dialysis Patient

Look for this icon to find recipes for the pre-dialysis patient

It is very important for people who have kidney disease but who are not on dialysis to be able to identify foods that may help or hinder reaching their nutrition goals. Your diet affects how you feel and may delay the progression of kidney failure. Your goal should be delaying the onset for the need of dialysis, minimizing failing kidney symptoms, such as uremia, and maintaining and/or achieving optimal nutritional health.

It will be important for you to understand how to eat well—how to get the right amount of protein or vitamin-enriched foods, maintain a healthy target weight, and manage your fluid balance.

Your doctor or dietitian may prescribe a renal diet that should take into account individual factors such as:
- Your treatment goals
- Your medical history
- Your current symptoms and condition
- Your particular likes and dislikes
- Your nutrition goals
- Your weight status
- MOST IMPORTANTLY—your nutrition lab results

The special dietary considerations behind this plan are designed to help you avoid foods with waste products that your compromised kidneys may have difficulty eliminating. You may need to regulate your intake of minerals such as sodium, potassium, phosphorus, and calcium. You will know if you should regulate your intake of these minerals based upon your lab results and how you feel.

You should also eat and drink as needed to regulate your fluid balance, which means regulating your intake of fluids, including alcohol.

Goals of the pre-dialysis diet:
- Cutting down the workload of your kidneys
- Helping to keep the kidney function that is left
- Reducing symptoms like fatigue, nausea, itching, and a bad taste in the mouth
- Controlling the effects of high blood sugars if you have diabetes
- Helping to control high blood pressure

It is important to follow the guidelines your doctor and/or dietitian give you. There are many kidney-friendly recipes that can help put these recommendations into practice.

General Diet Guidelines

Calcium: It's recommended that those ages 11 and up should consume about 1,000 mg of calcium daily. This includes calcium from all sources, both food and supplements.

Your intake should be based upon keeping your blood calcium levels between 8.4 and 10.2 mg/dl.

Phosphorus: Phosphorus in the diet may be restricted if blood levels reach greater than 4.6 mg/dl. Recommended intake is less than 1,200 mg/day if serum phosphorus levels are high. Foods high in phosphorus include dairy products, dark sodas, nuts and peanut butter, beer, legumes, organ meats, and chocolate.

A phosphate binder may also be initiated once levels reach greater than 4.6 mg/dl. If prescribed, these binders should be taken 10 minutes prior to or during meals.

Sodium: May be restricted with co-morbid diseases, like high blood pressure. Recommended intake is 2,000–3,000 mg/day.

Potassium: No need to change your dietary intake of potassium unless your serum potassium is out of range. Recommended intake is 2,000–3,000 mg/day. An optimal potassium level is 3.5–5.0 mg/dl.

Calories: Adequate to maintain an ideal body weight and nutrition status.

Fluid: Your fluid intake should be monitored by examining your individual fluid status. If you are retaining fluid, cut back on your intake and vice versa.

1. People with healthy kidneys should drink 8–10 eight ounce glasses (64 ounces) of water every day.
2. Signs of dehydration: headaches, heartburn, joint and back pain, kidney stones, constipation, and fatigue.
3. Drinking water lowers the risk for urinary tract and bladder infections, which can be common in kidney disease patients.
4. Signs of fluid overload include swollen fingers and ankles, high blood pressure, bloating, and difficulty breathing.

Protein: Recent literature does not support strict protein restrictions in this patient population. A recommended intake is 0.8 grams/kilogram of ideal body weight per day.

To calculate how much protein you should consume per day, follow the equation below.

First you need to figure out your Ideal Body Weight (IBW). To do this:

- Women – First 5 ft. = 100 lbs.; every inch above 5 feet, add 5 pounds
- Men – First 5 ft. = 106 lbs.; every inch above 5 feet, add 6 pounds

To calculate the amount of protein to eat per day:

1. Ideal Body Weight (insert your number) / 2.2 (kg) = Weight (kg)
2. Weight (kg) x .8 = g of protein to eat per day

Example: 5-foot-3 Woman

1. IBW = 100 lbs. + (3 x 5 lbs.) = 115 lbs.
2. 115 lbs./ 2.2 = 52.3 kg
3. 52.3 (kg) x .8 = 42 g of protein/day
4. Equates to 6 oz (1 oz = 7 g of protein)

*Recommended daily values include protein from dairy, grains, vegetables, and meat sources.

Other General Guidelines

Include Anti-inflammatory Foods

Call it too much of a good thing. Inflammation is the immune system's first line of defense in the war against infection and disease. A critical part of the healing process, the inflammatory response appears to possess an unfortunate sense of irony, sometimes overreacting and becoming the very thing it's supposed to destroy. Inflammation exacerbates most and probably all diseases, including kidney disease. Normally, inflammation is part of the body's immune response to injury or infection. Inflammation helps kill the germs that cause infections, and it also stimulates the healing process. The problem occurs when inflammation becomes chronic. Chronic inflammation starts breaking down the body or specific organs.

General Guidelines:

- Aim for variety
- Include as much fresh/organic food as possible
- Minimize your consumption of processed foods and fast foods
- Eat an abundance of fruits and vegetables

Include Essential Fatty Acids: Those fatty acids that are required in our daily diets

Omega 3's: Anti-inflammatory (cold water fish, flaxseed, leafy-green vegetables, walnuts)

General Diet Guidelines for the Hemodialysis Patient

Look for this icon to find recipes for the hemodialysis patient

Between dialysis treatments, wastes can build up in your blood and make you sick. You can reduce the amount of wastes by watching what you eat and drink. Your hemodialysis diet will most likely consist of:

Calcium: It's recommended that those ages 11 and up should consume about 1,000 mg of calcium daily. This includes calcium from all sources, both food and supplements.

Your intake should be based upon keeping your blood calcium levels between 8.4 and 9.5 mg/dl.

Phosphorus: If you have too much phosphorus in your blood, it can pull calcium from your bones. Also, too much phosphorus may make your skin itch. Phosphorus in the diet may be restricted if blood levels reach greater than 5.0 mg/dl. Recommended intake is less than 1,200 mg/day.

Foods high in phosphorus include: dairy products, dark sodas, nuts and peanut butter, beer, legumes, organ meats, and chocolate.

A phosphate binder will be initiated once levels reach greater than 5.0 mg/dl. If prescribed, these binders should be taken 10 minutes prior to or during meals.

Sodium: Too much sodium makes you thirsty. If you drink more fluid, your heart has to work harder to pump the fluid through the body. Your sodium will most likely be restricted to less than 2,000mg/day.

Fluid: Your fluid intake will most likely be restricted to 1–1.5 liters/day. Fluid can build up between dialysis sessions, causing swelling and weight gain. Too high a level of fluid gains can cause cramping and low blood pressure during the dialysis treatment.

Potassium: Potassium is a mineral that affects how steadily your heart beats. It is found in many foods, especially milk, fruits, and vegetables. Potassium levels can rise between dialysis sessions. Potassium is usually restricted to 2,340 mg/day.

Protein: Most people on dialysis are encouraged to eat as much high-quality protein as they can. The better nourished you are, the healthier you will be. You will be encouraged to eat approximately 1.2 grams of protein per kilogram of ideal body weight per day, at a minimum.

Calories: Adequate to maintain an ideal body weight and nutrition status.

Roasted Corn and Edamame Salad
page 31

General Diet Guidelines for the Peritoneal Dialysis Patient

Pd *Look for this icon to find recipes for the peritoneal dialysis patient*

For the most part, extensive dietary restrictions are not necessary for people on peritoneal dialysis. Your peritoneal dialysis diet will most likely consist of:

Calcium: It's recommended that those ages 11 and up should consume about 1,000 mg of calcium daily. This includes calcium from all sources, both food and supplements.

Your intake should be based upon keeping your blood calcium levels between 8.4 and 9.5 mg/dl.

Phosphorus: Like a hemodialysis patient, if you have too much phosphorus in your blood, it can pull calcium from your bones. Also, too much phosphorus may make your skin itch. Phosphorus in the diet may be restricted if blood levels reach greater than 5.0 mg/dl. Recommended intake is less than 1,200 mg/day.

Grilled Sweet Potatoes and Scallions
page 44

Foods high in phosphorus include: dairy products, dark sodas, nuts and peanut butter, beer, legumes, organ meats, and chocolate.

A phosphate binder will be initiated once levels reach greater than 5.0 mg/dl. If prescribed, these binders should be taken 10 minutes prior to or during meals.

Sodium: Because you are doing dialysis every day, sodium is not usually restricted. A good guideline to follow is to keep your sodium intake between 2,000 and 3,000 mg/day or less.

Fluid: Usually not restricted. Eating and drinking less sodium/fluids allows you to use lower sugar solutions for removing the sodium/fluid from your body. This will help prevent unwanted weight gain.

Potassium: Usually not restricted. Most patients on peritoneal dialysis have normal potassium levels and do not need to limit their intake of high-potassium foods.

Protein: Patients on peritoneal dialysis are advised to follow a high-protein diet because protein is lost through the dialysis. You will be encouraged to eat 1.2 to 1.4 grams of protein per kilogram of ideal body weight per day, at a minimum.

Calories: The dextrose in the peritoneal dialysis solution is used to remove extra fluid from your body. It is also a source of extra calories, which can lead to weight gain. If you have diabetes, it will be especially important to watch your carbohydrate intake.

Tr General Diet Guidelines for the Transplant Patient

Look for this icon to find recipes for the transplant patient

Once you have received a new kidney, your diet may resemble the one you ate before you got sick. It is still important to watch your sodium intake, especially if you have high blood pressure. Your doctor and dietitian will help you make the transition to your new diet and will ease up your restrictions once your new kidney proves it can do its job well.

Here are a few points to consider once you have received your new kidney:

- Prevent excess weight gain. Many people who have received a transplant gain weight because they have fewer restrictions on foods and feel well enough to eat. Gaining too much weight can increase your risk for hypertension and diabetes. Make sure you keep track of your weight and the number of calories you are eating, and participate in regular physical activity.

- Protect your bones. Kidney disease can weaken your bones. It is important to make sure you are eating adequate calcium and participating in weight-bearing activity. Talk to your doctor about receiving a bone scan to assess the health of your bones.

- Avoid dietary supplements that are used to boost the immune system such as Echinacea, Goldenseal, and Astragalus. These can interfere with your anti-rejection medication. Supplements that may be beneficial include fish oil (1 to 3 grams per day to help reduce the risk of heart disease), approved multivitamins, and calcium.

In addition, make sure that you wash your hands frequently and keep your countertops and dish towels clean. Throw your sponge into the dishwasher every night, and make sure to replace it when it starts to look worn.

While you are recovering from a transplant, good nutrition can help reduce recovery time, prevent complications, and improve your sense of well-being. Make sure you ask your doctor and dietitian to give you specific recommendations to help support your health through the process.

Easy Bruschetta
page 20

Because of medications you will be taking to help prevent rejection, your immune system may be weakened. One of your primary concerns regarding food will be safety. Avoid food-borne illness by keeping hot food hot and cold food cold. As a general rule, do not leave food out of the refrigerator for more than two hours, especially if it has multiple ingredients. When you finish a meal, make sure you put the food away quickly and reheat to the appropriate temperature (see thermometer diagram).

The following foods are known to be "potentially hazardous."

- Dairy products such as milk, cream, butter, and cheese
- Potato salad or macaroni salad
- Eggs, meat, poultry, and fish
- Custard-filled bakery items
- Tofu
- Sliced melons
- Cooked beans and rice
- Caesar salad dressing
- Mayonnaise

If these foods are mishandled they are likely to cause illness.

Safe Food Temperatures

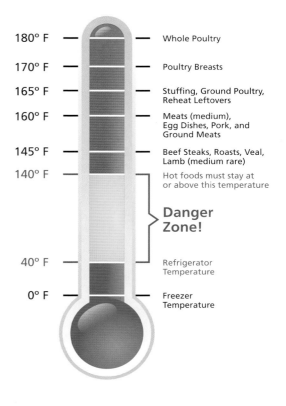

180° F	Whole Poultry
170° F	Poultry Breasts
165° F	Stuffing, Ground Poultry, Reheat Leftovers
160° F	Meats (medium), Egg Dishes, Pork, and Ground Meats
145° F	Beef Steaks, Roasts, Veal, Lamb (medium rare)
140° F	Hot foods must stay at or above this temperature

Danger Zone!

40° F	Refrigerator Temperature
0° F	Freezer Temperature

Easy Bruschetta

Appetizers

Every meal needs a starting point. So why not start here? These tasty treats are a great kick-off to any KidneyWise™ meal you want to make. Just make sure you don't spoil your dinner.

Artichoke Dip

Prep Time: 1 Hour
Servings: 10

Ingredients

- **1 cup frozen artichoke hearts**
- **¼ cup mayonnaise**
- **¼ cup sour cream**
- **2 tablespoons cream cheese**
- **2 teaspoons hot sauce**
- **1 large clove garlic, crushed**
- **1 tablespoon Parmesan cheese**

Per Serving

Calories:	55.62	Omega-3 (g):	0.16
Protein (g):	1.19	Omega-6 (g):	1.02
Carbohydrates (g):	3.41	Phosphorus (mg):	23.89
Dietary Fiber (g):	0.78	Potassium (mg):	59.79
Fat (g):	4.41	Sodium (mg):	94.88

Preparation

Preheat oven to 375° F. Place artichoke hearts in a saucepan, cover with water and bring to a boil. Reduce heat to medium, and cook for 6 minutes. Drain, and rinse with cold water to cool. Chop artichoke hearts. In a medium bowl, combine mayonnaise, sour cream, cream cheese, hot sauce and garlic. Stir in artichoke hearts. Transfer mixture to a baking dish. Top with Parmesan cheese. Place in oven, and bake for 30 minutes or until bubbly on top. If canned or jarred artichokes in water are used instead of frozen, look for the lowest-sodium brand. Rinse well to help reduce sodium. Try this dip on toasted slices of baguette, crisp celery, or with your favorite low-sodium crackers.

Crunchy Chicken Appetizers

Prep Time: 30 Minutes
Servings: 8

Ingredients

- **1 pound boneless skinless chicken breasts**
- **2 cups shredded whole wheat cereal biscuits, crushed**
- **½ teaspoon garlic powder**
- **1 egg**
- **¼ teaspoon salt**
- **¼ teaspoon ground black pepper**
- **½ cup (1 stick) margarine**
- **Spicy Brown Mustard (optional)**
- **Sweet and Sour Sauce (optional)**

Per Serving

Calories:	252.10	Omega-3 (g):	0.19
Protein (g):	16.55	Omega-6 (g):	3.83
Carbohydrates (g):	17.82	Phosphorus (mg):	213.84
Dietary Fiber (g):	2.24	Potassium (mg):	251.09
Fat (g):	13.07	Sodium (mg):	250.73

Preparation

Cut chicken into 1-inch-wide strips; set aside. Combine cereal crumbs and garlic powder in shallow bowl. Beat egg, salt and pepper in another shallow bowl with wire whisk until well blended. Dip chicken strips in egg mixture, then in crumb mixture, turning to evenly coat all sides. Melt margarine in large skillet over medium heat. Add chicken strips; cook 6 to 8 minutes or until golden brown and no longer pink in center, turning occasionally. Serve warm with spicy brown mustard and/or sweet and sour sauce.

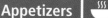

Barbecue Meatballs

Prep Time: 30 Minutes
Servings: 24

Pr He Pd Tr

Ingredients

- **3 pounds ground beef**
- **2 large eggs, beaten**
- **½ cup skim milk or nondairy milk substitute**
- **1 cup dry oatmeal flakes (Quaker® Quick Oats)**
- **½ cup diced onion**
- **1 tablespoon dried thyme**
- **1 teaspoon dried oregano**
- **½ teaspoon pepper**
- **1 cup barbecue sauce (look for the lowest-sodium brand or make your own)**
- **½ cup water**

Per Serving

Calories:	160.18	Omega-3 (g):	0.06
Protein (g):	11.33	Omega-6 (g):	0.29
Carbohydrates (g):	4.40	Phosphorus (mg):	101.85
Dietary Fiber (g):	0.80	Potassium (mg):	236.82
Fat (g):	10.53	Sodium (mg):	55.02

Preparation

Preheat oven to 375° F. Combine all ingredients, except barbecue sauce and water, in a large bowl, and mix together. Roll into 1-inch balls and place on a baking sheet. Bake for 10 to 15 minutes, until meatballs are cooked through.

Combine barbecue sauce and water in a warming dish on low temperature setting. Add meatballs, and stir. Cover until ready to serve.

....

Chili Lime Shrimp

Prep Time: 25 Minutes
Servings: 4

Pr He Pd Tr

Ingredients

- **2 tablespoons tomato paste**
- **2 tablespoons chili garlic paste**
- **PAM® No-Stick Cooking Spray**
- **1 pound medium shrimp (16 to 20 count), peeled, deveined**
- **1 lime, cut into wedges**

Per Serving

Calories:	46.34	Omega-3 (g):	0.13
Protein (g):	6.13	Omega-6 (g):	0.06
Carbohydrates (g):	5.09	Phosphorus (mg):	67.37
Dietary Fiber (g):	0.92	Potassium (mg):	165.78
Fat (g):	0.55	Sodium (mg):	118.01

Preparation

Combine tomato paste and chili paste in small bowl. Spray wok or large skillet with cooking spray; heat over high heat 1 minute. Add shrimp; cook 5 minutes or until shrimp turn pink, stirring frequently. Add tomato paste mixture; toss to evenly coat shrimp. Divide shrimp evenly among 4 serving plates. Squeeze 1 lime wedge over shrimp on each plate before serving. Serve with additional lime wedges.

Yucatan Lime Soup

Prep Time: 30 Minutes
Servings: 4

Pr Pd Tr

Ingredients

- 2 corn tortillas (6-inch diameter), cut into thin strips
- Vegetable oil spray
- 1 tablespoon olive oil
- ½ cup onion, finely chopped
- 8 cloves garlic, minced
- 2 Serrano chili peppers, thinly sliced
- 1 medium tomato, halved crosswise and seeded, with skin removed
- 4 cups no-salt-added chicken broth or homemade, salt-free stock
- 1 ½ cups cooked chicken breast, shredded
- 1 bay leaf
- ¼ cup lime juice
- ¼ cup fresh cilantro, chopped
- Ground black pepper to taste

Per Serving

Calories:	214.09	Omega-3 (g):	0.10
Protein (g):	23.12	Omega-6 (g):	1.15
Carbohydrates (g):	16.23	Phosphorus (mg):	259.61
Dietary Fiber (g):	2.02	Potassium (mg):	613.55
Fat (g):	7.20	Sodium (mg):	223.66

Not recommended for pre-dialysis patients on a potassium restriction.

Preparation

Preheat oven to 400° F. Arrange the tortilla strips on a baking sheet. Spray with vegetable oil spray. Bake for 3 minutes or until lightly toasted. Remove from oven and place onto a plate to cool. Heat oil in a large saucepan over medium heat. Add onion, garlic and chili peppers. Cook until the onion is translucent. Add tomato, broth, chicken, and bay leaf. Simmer for 8 to 10 minutes. Add lime juice and cilantro. Season with black pepper. Taste, and add more lime juice if desired. Serve with tortilla strips sprinkled on top.

Classic Deviled Eggs

Prep Time: 20 Minutes
Servings: 6

Pr He Pd Tr

Ingredients

- 6 peeled hard-cooked eggs
- 3 tablespoons mayonnaise
- 2 tablespoons plain yogurt
- 2 teaspoons Dijon mustard
- Squirt of lemon juice
- Paprika

Per Serving

Calories:	111.07	Omega-3 (g):	0.20
Protein (g):	6.63	Omega-6 (g):	1.87
Carbohydrates (g):	2.84	Phosphorus (mg):	94.90
Dietary Fiber (g):	0.12	Potassium (mg):	78.95
Fat (g):	12.83	Sodium (mg):	161.18

Preparation

Cut eggs in half, lengthwise. Remove the yolks, and blend them by hand with mayonnaise, yogurt, Dijon mustard, and lemon juice. Spoon the mixture back into the whites. Dust with paprika.

Eggplant Dip

Prep Time: 3 Hours
Servings: 4

Pr Pd Tr

Ingredients

- 1 ½ large eggplants, halved
- Olive oil cooking spray
- 1 tablespoon olive oil
- 1 spring onion, coarsely chopped
- 1 garlic clove, minced
- 1 ½ heirloom tomatoes, coarsely chopped
- ½ teaspoon hot paprika
- 1 tablespoon plus ½ teaspoon plain low-fat yogurt
- Coarsely ground black pepper
- 1 tablespoon plus ½ teaspoon thinly sliced basil

Per Serving

Calories:	110.61	Omega-3 (g):	0.07
Protein (g):	2.91	Omega-6 (g):	0.63
Carbohydrates (g):	15.06	Phosphorus (mg):	73.41
Dietary Fiber (g):	7.82	Potassium (mg):	612.56
Fat (g):	5.74	Sodium (mg):	12.52

Not recommended for pre-dialysis patients on a potassium restriction.

Preparation

Preheat oven to 350° F. Coat eggplants with cooking spray. Roast 1 hour. Scoop pulp into a sieve lined with cheese-cloth; drain 1 hour. Remove pulp; puree in food processor; transfer to a bowl. Heat oil in a sauté pan over medium heat. Cook onion 5 minutes or until soft. Add garlic; cook 3 minutes or until soft. Add tomatoes and paprika; cook 3 to 5 minutes. Let cool. Stir yogurt into eggplant puree; add onion and tomatoes. Season with pepper. Chill 30 minutes. Garnish with basil. Serve with raw vegetables.

Salsa

Prep Time: 20 Minutes
Servings: 4

Pr He Pd Tr

Ingredients

- 4 large plum tomatoes (about 1 pound), diced (to yield 2 cups)
- ¼ cup chopped white onion
- 3 tablespoons fresh cilantro, chopped
- 2 teaspoons minced jalapeno (remove seeds for less heat)
- 1 ½ teaspoons fresh lime juice
- 1 small garlic clove, minced

Per Serving

Calories:	19.27	Omega-3 (g):	0.00
Protein (g):	0.70	Omega-6 (g):	0.01
Carbohydrates (g):	4.38	Phosphorus (mg):	19.65
Dietary Fiber (g):	0.89	Potassium (mg):	163.22
Fat (g):	0.23	Sodium (mg):	6.40

Preparation

Combine all the ingredients in a bowl. If you prefer a smoother texture, more like jarred, pulse half the salsa in a food processor; then combine it with the remaining chunky half. Cover tightly, and refrigerate for up to 5 days.

Easy Bruschetta

Prep Time: 25 minutes
Servings: 8

Ingredients

- ½ cup chopped red bell pepper
- ½ cup chopped sun-dried tomatoes
- 2 tablespoons grated Romano cheese
- 2 tablespoons grated Parmesan cheese
- 1 tablespoon minced garlic
- 1 ½ teaspoons dried basil leaves
- 1 ½ teaspoons dried oregano leaves
- 1 can (14 ½ ounces) Hunt's® Petite Diced Tomatoes
- 1 baguette, cut into ½-inch diagonal slices, toasted
- Pepper to taste

Per Serving

Calories:	124.00	Omega-3 (g):	0.04
Protein (g):	4.86	Omega-6 (g):	0.31
Carbohydrates (g):	22.31	Phosphorus (mg):	83.91
Dietary Fiber (g):	2.40	Potassium (mg):	311.74
Fat (g):	2.04	Sodium (mg):	414.05

Preparation

Combine and mix all ingredients, except baguette slices, in a saucepan. Season with pepper to taste; bring to a boil. Reduce heat. Simmer 10 minutes. Serve at room temperature on toasted baguette slices.

Basil and Cream Cheese Spread

Prep Time: 2 Hours 15 Minutes (includes chill time)
Servings: 4

Ingredients

- PAM® for Baking Spray
- ¼ cup chopped walnuts
- 8 ounces light cream cheese, softened
- 2 tablespoons chopped fresh basil
- 2 cloves garlic, minced
- ½ teaspoon grated lemon peel
- 2 medium zucchini, sliced thin

Per Serving

Calories:	198.42	Omega-3 (g):	0.87
Protein (g):	8.47	Omega-6 (g):	3.11
Carbohydrates (g):	8.87	Phosphorus (mg):	149.21
Dietary Fiber (g):	1.69	Potassium (mg):	397.06
Fat (g):	15.06	Sodium (mg):	178.10

Not recommended for pre-dialysis patients on a potassium restriction.

Preparation

Preheat oven to 350° F. Coat an 8-inch square baking pan with cooking spray. Add walnuts, and bake for 5 to 7 minutes, or just until nuts begin to brown, stirring once or twice. Set aside. Combine cream cheese, basil, garlic and lemon peel in small mixing bowl. Stir in walnuts. Cover with plastic wrap. Chill 1 to 2 hours to blend flavors. Serve with zucchini slices.

Serving Suggestions

For a fresh look, line a shallow bowl with fresh basil leaves, and spoon cream cheese mixture in center, place the bowl on a serving plate, and arrange zucchini slices around the bowl.

Hot Crab Dip

Prep Time: 25 Minutes
Servings: 10

Pr He Pd Tr

Ingredients

- One 8-ounce package cream cheese, softened
- 1 tablespoon finely minced onion
- 1 teaspoon lemon juice
- 2 teaspoons Worcestershire sauce
- ⅛ teaspoon black pepper
- Cayenne pepper to taste
- 2 tablespoons nondairy creamer
- One 6-ounce can crab meat

Per Serving

Calories:	101.50	Omega-3 (g):	0.17
Protein (g):	5.25	Omega-6 (g):	0.19
Carbohydrates (g):	1.33	Phosphorus (mg):	70.84
Dietary Fiber (g):	0.03	Potassium (mg):	108.08
Fat (g):	8.42	Sodium (mg):	137.31

Preparation

Preheat oven to 375° F. Place softened cream cheese in a bowl. Add onion, lemon juice, Worcestershire sauce, black pepper and cayenne pepper. Mix well. Stir in nondairy creamer. Add crab meat and stir until blended. Place mixture into an oven-safe dish. Bake uncovered for 15 minutes or until hot and bubbly. Serve warm with low-sodium crackers.

Chickpeas and Balsamic Vinegar Bruschetta

Prep Time: 20 Minutes
Servings: 5

Pr Tr

Ingredients

- 1 15-ounce can chickpeas, drained, rinsed, and roughly chopped
- ½ cup fresh flat-leaf parsley leaves, roughly chopped
- ½ baguette
- 1 clove garlic, finely chopped
- 1 tablespoon extra-virgin olive oil
- 2 tablespoons balsamic vinegar
- ¼ teaspoon kosher salt
- ¼ teaspoon black pepper

Per Serving

Calories:	206.74	Omega-3 (g):	0.04
Protein (g):	6.69	Omega-6 (g):	0.43
Carbohydrates (g):	34.93	Phosphorus (mg):	107.96
Dietary Fiber (g):	4.75	Potassium (mg):	216.78
Fat (g):	4.49	Sodium (mg):	530.79

Preparation

Thinly slice half a baguette. Place the rounds on a baking sheet, and broil them until they're golden brown (about 1 ½ minutes per side). In a medium bowl, combine the chickpeas, parsley leaves, garlic, oil, balsamic vinegar, salt, and pepper. Spread the mixture on the rounds.

Golden Gazpacho

Prep Time: 2 Hours 15 Minutes
Servings: 4

Ingredients

- **1 ear fresh corn, shucked and rinsed (or ¾ cup frozen corn kernels, thawed)**
- **4 yellow tomatoes, seeded and finely diced**
- **½ small red onion, minced**
- **½ large yellow bell pepper, peeled, seeded finely diced**
- **½ large cucumber, peeled, seeded and finely diced**
- **¼ cup nonfat chicken (or vegetable) broth**
- **1 tablespoon chopped fresh parsley**
- **2 tablespoons extra-virgin olive oil**
- **¼ teaspoon coarse salt (kosher or sea salt)**
- **¼ teaspoon freshly ground black pepper**
- **¼ cup almonds**

Per Serving

Calories:	162.51	**Omega-3 (g):**	0.06
Protein (g):	4.77	**Omega-6 (g):**	1.48
Carbohydrates (g):	15.47	**Phosphorus (mg):**	143.70
Dietary Fiber (g): and	3.57	**Potassium (mg):**	778.93
Fat (g):	10.74	**Sodium (mg):**	249.44

Not recommended for pre-dialysis patients on a potassium restriction.

Preparation

Cut kernels off cob. (You can eat fresh corn raw; it provides crunchiness.) In a large bowl, combine corn, tomatoes, onion, bell pepper, cucumber, broth, parsley, oil, salt and black pepper. Cover, and refrigerate 2 hours. Before serving, toast almonds (10 minutes in a 350° F-oven). Serve soup cold, and garnish with toasted almonds and additional parsley.

Roast Beef Cocktail Sandwiches with Herb Butter

Prep Time: 20 Minutes
Servings: 24

Ingredients

- **1 stick unsalted butter, at room temperature**
- **2 tablespoons prepared horseradish (optional)**
- **¼ cup finely chopped fresh flat-leaf parsley leaves**
- **2 baguettes**
- **¾ pound thinly sliced roasted beef tenderloin or deli roast beef**

Per Serving

Calories:	133.65	**Omega-3 (g):**	0.05
Protein (g):	6.01	**Omega-6 (g):**	0.34
Carbohydrates (g):	10.97	**Phosphorus (mg):**	48.38
Dietary Fiber (g):	0.69	**Potassium (mg):**	63.95
Fat (g):	7.17	**Sodium (mg):**	138.07

Preparation

In a small bowl, combine the butter, horseradish, and parsley. Cut each baguette in half, lengthwise. Spread the butter on both sides of each baguette. Arrange the beef on the bottom half of the baguettes. Sandwich with the top half of the baguettes. Use a serrated knife to slice each baguette into 12 portions.

Tofu and Walnut-Stuffed Mushrooms

Pr Pd Tr

Prep Time: 1 Hour
Servings: 12

Ingredients

- **1 medium onion, diced small**
- **2 cloves garlic, peeled and finely chopped**
- **¼ cup olive oil**
- **14 ounces firm tofu, frozen and then defrosted (Freezing changes texture to a more meaty substance that soaks up flavor. Freeze in plastic wrap, thaw, and pat dry with paper towel to remove excess water.)**
- **½ teaspoon dried rosemary, crumbled**
- **2 small tomatoes, finely chopped**
- **⅓ cup ground walnuts**
- **2 teaspoons mellow miso, or more for stronger flavor (available at health-food stores)**
- **½ teaspoon balsamic vinegar**
- **2 tablespoons tomato paste**
- **Pepper to taste**
- **12 large, fresh cremini or white mushrooms, wiped clean, stems removed**
- **¼ cup chopped green onions**

Per Serving

Calories:	94.95	**Omega-3 (g):**	0.24
Protein (g):	4.28	**Omega-6 (g):**	1.87
Carbohydrates (g):	4.27	**Phosphorus (mg):**	78.62
Dietary Fiber (g):	1.31	**Potassium (mg):**	217.67
Fat (g):	7.53	**Sodium (mg):**	63.49

Preparation

Preheat oven to 350° F. In a large skillet, sauté onion and garlic in 2 tablespoons oil, until tender. Crumble tofu over onion and sauté another 5 minutes. Add rosemary and tomatoes and cook on low heat about 10 minutes or until mixture is fairly dry. Add walnuts, miso, vinegar, tomato paste and pepper to taste. Drizzle remaining 2 tablespoons oil over mixture. Place mushrooms in a baking dish, and fill each with about 1 tablespoon stuffing, using a spoon and pressing firmly to pack. Bake 20 minutes. Remove, and top each hors d'oeuvre with a sprinkle of green onion. Serve warm.

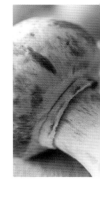

White Bean and Artichoke Dip

Pr Pd Tr

Prep Time: 20 Minutes
Makes: 2 ½ Cups

Ingredients

- **1 clove garlic, peeled**
- **1 teaspoon dried rosemary**
- **3 tablespoons fresh lemon juice**
- **2 cans (15.5 oz each) white beans (drained and rinsed)**
- **1 can (14 oz) artichoke hearts (packed in water, drained)**
- **Pepper to taste**

Per Serving

Calories:	61.73	**Omega-3 (g):**	0.00
Protein (g):	3.86	**Omega-6 (g):**	0.01
Carbohydrates (g):	12.01	**Phosphorus (mg):**	58.26
Dietary Fiber (g):	3.22	**Potassium (mg):**	276.94
Fat (g):	0.17	**Sodium (mg):**	20.93

Preparation

Place garlic and rosemary in a food processor, and finely chop. Add lemon juice and blend. Add beans and artichoke hearts and puree until smooth, stopping the machine a few times to scrape down the sides. Pepper to taste. Serve with carrot and celery sticks and/or pita bread (not potato chips!). Dip will keep refrigerated for 2 to 3 days.

Tomato Bread with Prosciutto

Prep Time: 1 Hour
Servings: 16

Ingredients

- **8 ripe plum tomatoes**
- **Salt and freshly ground pepper**
- **6 cloves garlic, finely chopped**
- **½ cup Spanish olive oil, divided**
- **¼ cup pine nuts**
- **1 tablespoon finely chopped fresh thyme leaves**
- **16 (½-inch-thick) slices Ciabatta or crusty country-style bread**
- **16 thin slices prosciutto**

Per Serving

Calories:	205.54	**Omega-3 (g):**	0.09
Protein (g):	7.78	**Omega-6 (g):**	1.72
Carbohydrates (g):	17.92	**Phosphorus (mg):**	94.09
Dietary Fiber (g):	1.68	**Potassium (mg):**	199.38
Fat (g):	11.56	**Sodium (mg):**	550.71

Preparation

Preheat grill to high. Brush tomatoes with olive oil, and season with salt and pepper. Place on the grill, and grill until charred on all sides. Coarsely chop the tomatoes, and then place in a food processor with the garlic, ¼ cup of the olive oil and the pine nuts. Process until smooth. Transfer to a bowl, stir in the thyme, and season with pepper, to taste. Let stand at room temperature for 30 minutes.

Brush each slice of bread with the remaining olive oil on both sides, season with pepper, and grill until lightly golden brown, about 30 seconds on each side. Remove the bread from the grill, brush 1 side of each slice with the pureed tomato mixture, and top each with a slice of prosciutto. Serve warm.

Roast Herb Artichokes

Prep Time: 45 Minutes
Servings: 5

Ingredients

- **16 fresh baby artichokes**
- **1 cup fresh flat-leaf parsley leaves, chopped**
- **3 cloves garlic, finely chopped**
- **¼ cup olive oil**
- **¼ teaspoon black pepper**
- **¼ cup water**
- **1 teaspoon grated lemon zest**
- **Mayonnaise, for serving (optional)**

Per Serving

Calories:	294.93	**Omega-3 (g):**	0.16
Protein (g):	13.85	**Omega-6 (g):**	1.20
Carbohydrates (g):	44.42	**Phosphorus (mg):**	340.18
Dietary Fiber (g):	21.24	**Potassium (mg):**	1435.13
Fat (g):	11.52	**Sodium (mg):**	372.22

Preparation

Preheat oven to 400° F. Trim the top ¼ of each artichoke. Remove and discard the tough, dark-green outer leaves until you can see the pale-green heart underneath. Trim the entire stem. Cut each artichoke in half, lengthwise. In a large cast-iron skillet, combine the parsley, garlic, oil, pepper and ¼ cup water. Add the artichokes and toss. Roast, stirring twice, until the artichokes are tender, about 30 minutes. Sprinkle with the zest. Serve with the mayonnaise (if desired).

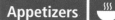
Mango Salsa Wontons

Prep Time: 45 Minutes
Servings: 24

Pr He Pd Tr

Ingredients

- Vegetable-oil cooking spray
- 24 wonton sheets (1 package; available at supermarkets or specialty stores)
- 1 large ripe mango, peeled, pitted and diced
- 1 small cucumber, peeled, seeded and diced
- ½ medium red onion, finely diced
- 2 to 3 tablespoons fresh lime juice
- 1 tablespoon olive oil
- Pinch of cayenne pepper
- 2 to 3 tablespoons chopped fresh cilantro (or more to taste)

Per Serving

Calories:	36.70	Omega-3 (g):	0.01
Protein (g):	0.94	Omega-6 (g):	0.10
Carbohydrates (g):	6.73	Phosphorus (mg):	10.76
Dietary Fiber (g):	0.41	Potassium (mg):	44.14
Fat (g):	0.74	Sodium (mg):	46.94

Preparation

Preheat oven to 350° F. Coat mini-muffin pans with cooking spray, and line the molds with wonton sheets. Bake for 9 to 12 minutes or until golden brown. Cool. Combine remaining ingredients in a large bowl. Fill each wonton with salsa and serve.

Grilled Guacamole

Prep Time: 1 Hour 20 Minutes
Servings: 24

Pr Pd Tr

Ingredients

- PAM® for Grilling Spray
- 4 ripe avocados, sliced in half, seed removed
- 1 can (10 ounces) diced tomatoes and green chilies, drained
- 5 green onions, chopped
- ¼ cup chopped fresh cilantro
- ½ teaspoon garlic salt (or garlic powder to lower sodium)
- ¼ teaspoon ground cumin
- Corn tortilla chips

Per Serving

Calories:	131.38	Omega-3 (g):	0.05
Protein (g):	2.28	Omega-6 (g):	1.36
Carbohydrates (g):	15.36	Phosphorus (mg):	72.33
Dietary Fiber (g):	3.28	Potassium (mg):	238.92
Fat (g):	7.38	Sodium (mg):	238.05

Preparation

Spray grate of outdoor grill and utensils with PAM® for Grilling Spray. Preheat grill to medium heat. Grill avocados, cut side down, 5 minutes or until browned. Cool; remove from skin, and coarsely chop. Combine chopped avocado with tomatoes, green onion, cilantro, garlic salt and cumin in small bowl. Refrigerate 1 hour before serving. Serve with tortilla chips, if desired.

Hearts of Palm
Salad with Ruby
Red Grapefruit and
Dungeness Crab

Salads

Push away those misguided thoughts of boring, bland salads. Not only do these salads taste great, they'll keep you on track for kidney health. Not even Popeye made spinach look this good.

Asian Cabbage Slaw

Prep Time: 15 Minutes
Servings: 8

Ingredients

- **1 head of cabbage, shredded**
- **4–8 green onions, finely diced (the more, the spicier)**
- **½ cup canned, sliced water chestnuts, drained**
- **1 tablespoon sugar**
- **¼ cup apple cider vinegar**
- **1 cup canola oil or olive oil**
- **2 tablespoons sesame seeds**
- **1 cup chow mein noodles**
- **Black pepper to taste**

Per Serving

Calories:	321.29		**Omega-3 (g):**	0.37
Protein (g):	2.76		**Omega-6 (g):**	3.86
Carbohydrates (g):	13.51		**Phosphorus (mg):**	56.10
Dietary Fiber (g):	3.64		**Potassium (mg):**	336.45
Fat (g):	29.98		**Sodium (mg):**	47.90

Preparation

Place shredded cabbage, green onions and water chestnuts in large bowl. Dissolve sugar in vinegar. Pour vinegar into oil, and whisk until mixed. Pour over cabbage mixture. Toss to evenly distribute the dressing. Chill several hours or overnight. Add chow mein noodles, sesame seeds, and pepper. Toss before serving.

Spinach, Apple and Walnut Salad

Prep Time: 20 Minutes
Servings: 4

Ingredients

- **2 Golden Delicious apples, cored, cut into large dice**
- **4 tablespoons lemon juice**
- **2 (5-ounce) packages (8 cups) baby spinach leaves**
- **3 tablespoons extra-virgin olive oil**
- **1 tablespoon apple cider vinegar**
- **2 tablespoons honey**
- **Freshly ground pepper to taste**
- **⅔ cup crumbled goat cheese**
- **½ cup chopped walnuts, toasted**

Per Serving

Calories:	368.81		**Omega-3 (g):**	1.52
Protein (g):	9.87		**Omega-6 (g):**	6.71
Carbohydrates (g):	29.66		**Phosphorus (mg):**	171.24
Dietary Fiber (g):	5.17		**Potassium (mg):**	608.98
Fat (g):	26.09		**Sodium (mg):**	162.58

Not recommended for pre-dialysis patients on a potassium restriction.

Preparation

Toss apples with 2 tablespoons of the lemon juice. Place spinach in a large bowl; remove long stems and bruised leaves. Whisk together remaining juice, olive oil, vinegar, honey, and ground pepper to taste. Toss spinach with apples and dressing. Divide among four bowls. Top with cheese and walnuts.

Crunchy Couscous Salad
Prep Time: 1 Hour 30 Minutes
Servings: 6

Pr He Pd Tr

Ingredients

Salad
- ¾ cup water
- ½ cup dry couscous
- 1 cup cucumbers, thinly sliced and quartered
- ½ cup red bell pepper, chopped
- ¼ cup sweet onion, chopped
- 2 tablespoons black olives, chopped
- ¼ cup flat-leaf parsley, chopped

Dressing
- 4 teaspoons olive oil
- 1 tablespoon white wine or unseasoned rice vinegar
- 2 tablespoons crumbled feta cheese
- 1 teaspoon dried basil
- ⅛ teaspoon salt
- ⅛ teaspoon pepper

Per Serving

Calories:	105.62	**Omega-3 (g):**	0.04
Protein (g):	2.81	**Omega-6 (g):**	0.33
Carbohydrates (g):	14.50	**Phosphorus (mg):**	50.15
Dietary Fiber (g):	1.55	**Potassium (mg):**	122.99
Fat (g):	4.17	**Sodium (mg):**	113.51

Preparation

In a medium saucepan, heat water to a boil, and add couscous. Return to boiling. Remove pan from heat, cover, and let stand for 5 minutes. Fluff with a fork, and let cool while preparing vegetables. Add cucumber, bell pepper, onion, olives and parsley to couscous. Combine olive oil, wine or vinegar, feta cheese, basil, salt and pepper to make dressing. Mix with the couscous salad. Refrigerate at least 1 hour. Serve chilled.

Roasted Corn
and Edamame
Salad

Roasted Corn and Edamame Salad

Prep Time: 1 Hour
Servings: 6

Pr He Pd Tr

Ingredients

- **2 ears fresh corn, with husks, or 1 ¼ cups cooked corn kernels**
- **½ cup shelled edamame**
- **¼ cup chopped red onion**
- **¼ cup small-diced red bell pepper**
- **1 tablespoon finely chopped fresh cilantro**
- **1 tablespoon light mayonnaise**
- **1 tablespoon lemon juice**
- **1 ½ teaspoons finely chopped or grated ginger**
- **⅛ teaspoon salt**
- **⅛ teaspoon freshly ground black pepper**

Per Serving

Calories:	51.59	**Omega-3 (g):**	0.04
Protein (g):	2.66	**Omega-6 (g):**	0.22
Carbohydrates (g):	8.06	**Phosphorus (mg):**	43.39
Dietary Fiber (g):	1.47	**Potassium (mg):**	162.26
Fat (g):	1.60	**Sodium (mg):**	89.86

Preparation

Soak fresh corn in cold water about 30 minutes. Heat grill on high. Grill corn in husks, 10 to 15 minutes, turning once. Let cool. Remove husks. Cut corn from cobs into a bowl; combine with remaining ingredients. Cover and chill in refrigerator until ready to serve.

Taco Pasta Salad

Prep Time: 1 Hour 30 Minutes
Servings: 8

Pr Pd Tr

Ingredients

- **12 ounces penne pasta, uncooked**
- **½ cup sour cream**
- **½ cup salsa**
- **2 tablespoons hot taco sauce, canned or bottled**
- **1 large garlic clove, minced**
- **½ cup canned green chilies, chopped**
- **3 tablespoons sliced black olives**
- **2 green onions, sliced**
- **½ cup red bell pepper, chopped**
- **½ cup Mexican cheese, shredded**
- **8 cups iceberg lettuce, shredded**

Per Serving

Calories:	231.75	**Omega-3 (g):**	0.11
Protein (g):	7.69	**Omega-6 (g):**	0.19
Carbohydrates (g):	35.94	**Phosphorus (mg):**	128.43
Dietary Fiber (g):	2.81	**Potassium (mg):**	328.24
Fat (g):	6.55	**Sodium (mg):**	376.52

Preparation

Cook the pasta according to package directions (omit salt). Drain and rinse until cooled. In a small bowl, combine sour cream and salsa. Mix into the pasta. Add hot taco sauce, garlic, chilies and olives to pasta and stir. Sprinkle green onions and bell pepper over top of pasta mixture. Cover, and refrigerate to chill. Before serving, sprinkle cheese on top of pasta salad. For each serving, put 1 cup shredded lettuce on a salad plate. Top lettuce bed with pasta salad.

Mock Potato Salad

Prep Time: 30 Minutes
Servings: 10

Pr He Pd Tr

Ingredients

- **1 cup uncooked rice or salad pasta (elbow, mini shells, salad macaroni)**
- **1 ¼ cups mayonnaise or salad dressing**
- **2 cups sliced celery**
- **1 medium purple (sweet) onion, finely chopped**
- **4 teaspoons prepared mustard**
- **4 hard-cooked eggs, chopped**
- **8 radishes, sliced**
- **1 cucumber, pared and diced**

Per Serving

Calories:	230.87	**Omega-3 (g):**	0.62
Protein (g):	4.73	**Omega-6 (g):**	5.02
Carbohydrates (g):	25.85	**Phosphorus (mg):**	83.87
Dietary Fiber (g):	1.13	**Potassium (mg):**	179.90
Fat (g):	12.22	**Sodium (mg):**	278.53

Preparation

Cook rice or pasta according to package directions, without added salt. Refrigerate to chill. Add mayonnaise, celery, onion and mustard to chilled rice or pasta. Mix well, and refrigerate until ready to serve. Stir in eggs, radish slices and cucumber before serving chilled salad.

Spinach-Mandarin Salad

Prep Time: 20 Minutes
Servings: 5

Pr He Pd Tr

Ingredients

- **2 cups fresh spinach (and/or leaf lettuce), washed and torn into large pieces**
- **½ cup dried, sweetened cranberries**
- **5-ounce can water chestnuts, drained**
- **¼ cup Chinese noodles**
- **1 cup apple wedges, cut in half**
- **1 cup mandarin oranges, drained**
- **1 teaspoon pepper**
- **¼-cup vinaigrette salad dressing**

Per Serving

Calories:	102.29	**Omega-3 (g):**	0.07
Protein (g):	1.24	**Omega-6 (g):**	0.39
Carbohydrates (g):	23.47	**Phosphorus (mg):**	27.76
Dietary Fiber (g):	3.53	**Potassium (mg):**	210.33
Fat (g):	1.07	**Sodium (mg):**	23.21

Preparation

Place washed, drained spinach leaves into a 1-quart serving bowl. Sprinkle dried cranberries over top. Add water chestnuts, Chinese noodles, apple wedges and mandarin oranges. Sprinkle pepper over top. Cover, and refrigerate to chill.

Toss lightly with ¼-cup vinaigrette salad dressing and serve.

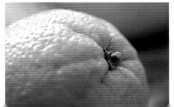

Grilled Vegetable Salad with Tofu
Prep Time: 50 Minutes
Servings: 4

Pr Pd Tr

Ingredients

Salad
- **1 zucchini, halved lengthwise**
- **1 ear corn, husked**
- **1 bunch asparagus (about 16 pencil-thin spears), ends trimmed**
- **1 (4-ounce) package firm tofu, cut into 2 ½-inch slices**
- **4 scallions**
- **Olive oil cooking spray**
- **Pepper to taste**
- **1 romaine heart, chopped**
- **¼ avocado, cut into bite-sized chunks**
- **1 cup mixed greens**

Dressing
- **1 teaspoon Dijon mustard**
- **1 teaspoon fresh lemon juice**
- **1 teaspoon fresh lime juice**
- **½ teaspoon white wine vinegar**
- **½ cup extra-virgin olive oil**

Per Serving

Calories:	248.10	**Omega-3 (g):**	0.37
Protein (g):	6.85	**Omega-6 (g):**	3.39
Carbohydrates (g):	16.42	**Phosphorus (mg):**	152.29
Dietary Fiber (g):	5.90	**Potassium (mg):**	682.21
Fat (g):	61.69	**Sodium (mg):**	41.46

Not recommended for pre-dialysis patients on a potassium restriction.

Preparation

Heat grill to medium. Spray zucchini, corn, asparagus, tofu and scallions with oil. Season with pepper. Grill scallions 2 minutes per side; tofu 2 minutes per side; zucchini and asparagus 3 minutes per side; corn 8 to 10 minutes, turning often. Cut zucchini and asparagus into bite-size pieces. Cut corn into chunks; slice off some kernels. Slice tofu into triangles. Combine veggies, tofu and remaining ingredients in a bowl.

Dressing

Combine all ingredients in a bowl; whisk until smooth. Divide salad greens and veggies between 2 bowls; drizzle each with 2 tablespoons dressing.

Watercress and Mushroom Salad with Lime Vinaigrette

`Pr` `Pd` `Tr`

Prep Time: 15 Minutes
Servings: 4

Ingredients

- **1 teaspoon Dijon mustard**
- **1 teaspoon red wine vinegar**
- **1 tablespoon lime juice**
- **¼ cup olive oil**
- **¼ teaspoon kosher salt**
- **Black pepper**
- **1 bunch watercress (about 4 cups)**
- **4 white mushrooms, thinly sliced (about ¼ pound)**

Per Serving

Calories:	131.32	**Omega-3 (g):**	0.12
Protein (g):	1.73	**Omega-6 (g):**	1.29
Carbohydrates (g):	1.86	**Phosphorus (mg):**	46.18
Dietary Fiber (g):	0.57	**Potassium (mg):**	208.28
Fat (g):	13.67	**Sodium (mg):**	174.92

Preparation

In a large bowl, whisk together Dijon mustard, vinegar, lime juice, olive oil, salt and a few grinds of black pepper. Add watercress and mushrooms, and toss.

Hearts of Palm Salad with Ruby Red Grapefruit and Dungeness Crab

`Pr`

Prep Time: 1 Hour 15 Minutes
Servings: 2

Ingredients

Dressing
- **¾ cup extra-virgin olive oil**
- **¼ cup fresh lemon juice**
- **1 tablespoon honey**
- **Pinch of freshly ground white pepper**

Salad
- **1 cup hearts of palm, cut into ¼-inch slices**
- **1 bunch organic watercress**
- **6 ounces precooked Dungeness crab meat**
- **1 tablespoon coarsely chopped cilantro**
- **1 tablespoon julienned basil**
- **1 tablespoon julienned mint**
- **Pinch of freshly ground white pepper**
- **2 ruby red grapefruit, peel and pith removed, segmented and segments cut into 4 pieces each**

Per Serving

Calories:	980.44	**Omega-3 (g):**	0.67
Protein (g):	23.73	**Omega-6 (g):**	7.53
Carbohydrates (g):	43.01	**Phosphorus (mg):**	242.28
Dietary Fiber (g):	5.88	**Potassium (mg):**	1077.58
Fat (g):	82.89	**Sodium (mg):**	646.23

Not recommended for pre-dialysis patients on a potassium restriction.

Preparation

Whisk together all dressing ingredients in a bowl. Marinate hearts of palm in ¾ cup of the dressing in another bowl for at least 1 hour. Divide watercress between 2 plates; top each pile with hearts of palm. In another bowl, mix crab meat, herbs and 1 teaspoon of the dressing. Season with pepper; toss until thoroughly mixed. Divide seasoned crab between 2 plates of watercress. Top with grapefruit pieces.

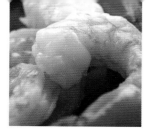

Shrimp Salad

Prep Time: 45 Minutes
Servings: 2

Pr Pd Tr

Ingredients

Shrimp Boil
- ¼ cup dry white wine
- ¼ teaspoon mustard seeds
- ⅛ teaspoon red pepper flakes or to taste
- 1 bay leaf
- 2 teaspoons lemon zest
- ½ pound medium-sized shrimp, peeled and deveined

Dressing
- 1 tablespoon extra-virgin olive oil
- 1 tablespoon white wine vinegar
- 1 teaspoon water
- 1 teaspoon fresh dill, chopped
- 1 teaspoon fresh oregano, chopped
- 1 teaspoon fresh basil, thinly sliced
- 1 garlic clove, finely minced
- ¼ teaspoon Dijon mustard
- 1 scallion, thinly sliced

Salad
- 2 cups green leaf lettuce pieces
- 4 cherry tomatoes
- 4 small mushrooms, sliced
- 2 slices crusty French or Italian bread

Per Serving

Calories:	401.01	**Omega-3 (g):**	0.70
Protein (g):	30.51	**Omega-6 (g):**	1.27
Carbohydrates (g):	39.58	**Phosphorus (mg):**	347.40
Dietary Fiber (g):	3.75	**Potassium (mg):**	535.09
Fat (g):	11.09	**Sodium (mg):**	580.54

Preparation

In medium saucepan, combine wine, mustard seeds, pepper flakes, bay leaf and lemon zest. Add enough water to fill pan ⅔ full. Bring mixture to a boil. Add shrimp and cook until pink, 3 to 4 minutes. Drain, rinse with cool water, and chill in the refrigerator. To make dressing, mix olive oil, vinegar, water, dill, oregano, basil, garlic, mustard and scallion in a salad shaker or screw-top jar. Shake well. Place shrimp in a bowl, add dressing, and toss well.

Serve shrimp over green leafy lettuce. Garnish each salad with two cherry tomatoes and 2 thinly sliced mushrooms. Serve with a slice of crusty French or Italian bread.

Roasted
Vegetable Salad

Roasted Vegetable Salad

Prep Time: 1 Hour 30 Minutes
Servings: 6

Ingredients

- **4 fresh ears of corn**
- **½ cup bottled reduced-calorie clear Italian salad dressing**
- **2 cups shredded fresh spinach**
- **2 cups red and/or yellow cherry tomatoes, halved**
- **2 teaspoons snipped fresh oregano or basil**
- **2 tablespoons finely shredded Parmesan cheese**
- **Fresh oregano or basil leaves (optional)**

Per Serving

Calories:	130.45	**Omega-3 (g):**	0.09
Protein (g):	1.80	**Omega-6 (g):**	0.89
Carbohydrates (g):	11.14	**Phosphorus (mg):**	53.02
Dietary Fiber (g):	1.68	**Potassium (mg):**	354.57
Fat (g):	9.26	**Sodium (mg):**	5.72

Not recommended for pre-dialysis patients on a potassium restriction.

Preparation

Remove husks and silks from corn. Brush with some of the salad dressing. Grill on the rack of an uncovered grill directly over medium heat for 15 to 20 minutes or until tender, turning often. (Or place in a shallow baking pan; bake in a 425° F oven for 30 minutes, turning once.) When corn is cool enough to handle, cut kernels from cobs (you should have about 2 cups kernels). In a large bowl, combine corn kernels, spinach, tomatoes and snipped herb. Add remaining salad dressing; toss gently to coat. To serve, spoon corn mixture into 6 small mugs or bowls. Sprinkle with Parmesan cheese. If desired, top with oregano leaves.

Fennel Salad with Fresh Mozzarella

Prep Time: 20 Minutes
Servings: 4

Ingredients

- **1 tablespoon sour cream**
- **1 teaspoon lemon juice**
- **3 tablespoons olive oil**
- **¼ teaspoon kosher salt**
- **⅛ teaspoon freshly ground black pepper**
- **1 fennel bulb, trimmed and very thinly sliced**
- **½ small red onion, peeled and thinly sliced**
- **1 red chili pepper, seeded and thinly sliced**
- **1 tablespoon fresh dill, chopped**
- **½ pound fresh mozzarella cheese, cut into ¼-inch slices**

Per Serving

Calories:	297.58	**Omega-3 (g):**	0.20
Protein (g):	15.99	**Omega-6 (g):**	1.23
Carbohydrates (g):	1.87	**Phosphorus (mg):**	340.38
Dietary Fiber (g):	2.35	**Potassium (mg):**	369.81
Fat (g):	22.32	**Sodium (mg):**	478.79

Not recommended for pre-dialysis patients on a potassium restriction.

Preparation

In a large bowl, whisk together the first 5 ingredients. Add the fennel, red onion, chili pepper and dill, and toss well. Divide the mozzarella slices evenly among 4 plates, and top with the dressed fennel.

Zucchini Ribbon Salad

Prep Time: 20 Minutes
Servings: 6

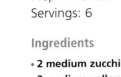

Ingredients

- **2 medium zucchini**
- **2 medium yellow squash**
- **2 tablespoons rice wine vinegar**
- **1 tablespoon sesame oil**
- **¼ teaspoon sugar**
- **⅛ teaspoon red pepper flakes**
- **½ teaspoon sesame seeds**
- **3 tablespoons low sodium soy sauce**
- **Freshly ground pepper to taste**

Per Serving

Calories:	51.45	Omega-3 (g):	0.08
Protein (g):	2.45	Omega-6 (g):	1.03
Carbohydrates (g):	5.97	Phosphorus (mg):	51.51
Dietary Fiber (g):	1.48	Potassium (mg):	344.87
Fat (g):	2.65	Sodium (mg):	279.00

Not recommended for pre-dialysis patients on a potassium restriction.

Preparation

Peel long ribbons of the zucchini and squash. In a large bowl, whisk together the remaining ingredients. Add the zucchini and squash, and toss to mix well. Season to taste with freshly ground pepper.

Strawberry Spinach Salad

Prep Time: 30 Minutes
Servings: 6

Ingredients

- **3 cups fresh spinach or 6-ounce package of pre-washed spinach**
- **1 cup fresh strawberries, thinly sliced**
- **1 tablespoon vinegar**
- **1 tablespoon lemon juice**
- **2 tablespoons honey**
- **⅛ teaspoon dry mustard powder**
- **3 tablespoons vegetable oil**

Per Serving

Calories:	94.72	Omega-3 (g):	0.12
Protein (g):	0.63	Omega-6 (g):	3.67
Carbohydrates (g):	8.62	Phosphorus (mg):	13.86
Dietary Fiber (g):	0.87	Potassium (mg):	129.68
Fat (g):	6.94	Sodium (mg):	12.44

Preparation

Wash and dry the spinach leaves. Tear into bite-sized pieces, and place in a bowl. Top spinach with sliced strawberries. Mix together the vinegar, lemon juice, honey, mustard powder and oil. Pour dressing over spinach and strawberries. Toss well, and serve immediately.

Chicken Salad with Apple and Basil

Prep Time: 45 Minutes

Servings: 4

Ingredients

- **4 boneless, skinless chicken breasts**
- **½ teaspoon kosher salt**
- **1 teaspoon black pepper**
- **¼ cup fresh lime juice (2 to 3 limes)**
- **1 tablespoon white wine vinegar or rice vinegar**
- **2 tablespoons light brown sugar**
- **4 scallions (white and light green parts), thinly sliced**
- **2 Granny Smith apples (peeled, if desired), diced**
- **2 tablespoons thinly sliced fresh mint**
- **½ cup thinly sliced fresh basil**

Per Serving

Calories:	290.84	**Omega-3 (g):**	0.10
Protein (g):	37.21	**Omega-6 (g):**	2.47
Carbohydrates (g):	20.93	**Phosphorus (mg):**	332.62
Dietary Fiber (g):	2.38	**Potassium (mg):**	366.64
Fat (g):	3.24	**Sodium (mg):**	370.88

Preparation

Rinse the chicken, and pat it dry with paper towels. Pound it to an even thickness. Place the chicken in a large saucepan, and add enough water to cover by ½ inch. Add ½ teaspoon of the salt and ½ teaspoon of the pepper, and bring to a gentle simmer. Cook until no trace of pink remains, 8 to 10 minutes. Transfer the chicken to a bowl of ice water for 5 minutes.

Meanwhile, in a large bowl, combine the lime juice, vinegar and sugar, stirring until the sugar dissolves. Add the scallions and apples, and toss.

Drain the chicken, and pat it dry. Dice the chicken, and add it to the apple mixture along with the mint, basil and remaining pepper. Toss, and divide among individual plates.

New Potato Salad

Prep Time: 1 Hour 15 Minutes

Servings: 5

Ingredients

- **16 small new potatoes (5 cups), pre-soaked for 3 hours**
- **2 tablespoons olive oil**
- **¼ cup green onions, chopped**
- **¼ teaspoon black pepper**
- **1 teaspoon dill weed, dried**

Per Serving

Calories:	468.59	**Omega-3 (g):**	0.10
Protein (g):	11.13	**Omega-6 (g):**	0.67
Carbohydrates (g):	95.49	**Phosphorus (mg):**	312.93
Dietary Fiber (g):	12.19	**Potassium (mg):**	1155.36
Fat (g):	5.91	**Sodium (mg):**	33.46

Not recommended for pre-dialysis patients on a potassium restriction.

Preparation

Thoroughly clean potatoes with vegetable brush and water. Boil potatoes for 20 minutes or until tender. Drain and cool potatoes for 20 minutes. Cut potatoes into quarters and mix with olive oil, onions, and spices. Refrigerate until ready to serve.

Tuna Veggie Salad

Prep Time: 45 Minutes
Servings: 4

Ingredients

- ¾ cup water
- ½ cup red bell pepper, diced
- ½ cup green bell pepper, diced
- 1 cup zucchini, thinly sliced
- 1 can (6 ounces) tuna packed in water, drained
- ¼ cup green onions with tops, chopped
- ¼ cup fresh basil, chopped
- 2 ½ tablespoons red wine vinegar
- 1 tablespoon olive oil
- ½ teaspoon fresh garlic, minced
- ⅛ teaspoon black pepper

Per Serving

Calories:	96.40	Omega-3 (g):	0.18
Protein (g):	11.73	Omega-6 (g):	0.37
Carbohydrates (g):	4.08	Phosphorus (mg):	93.04
Dietary Fiber (g):	1.34	Potassium (mg):	278.33
Fat (g):	3.89	Sodium (mg):	148.94

Preparation

Pour ¾ cup of water into a medium saucepan. Place diced bell peppers and sliced zucchini into a steamer basket, and place over the saucepan. Heat water to a boil, and steam vegetables for 10 minutes. Remove vegetables from heat, drain off any excess water, and transfer to a serving bowl. Add tuna, green onions and basil. Toss to combine ingredients. To make dressing, combine vinegar, oil, garlic and black pepper in a jar with a tight-fitting lid and shake well. Pour dressing over tuna and vegetable mixture, and mix well.

Arugula Salad

Prep Time: 15 Minutes
Servings: 1

Ingredients

- 1 cup arugula
- 1 clementine, broken into sections
- ½ cup shaved Parmesan cheese
- 1 teaspoon white wine vinegar
- 2 teaspoons extra-virgin olive oil
- ⅛ teaspoon black pepper

Per Serving

Calories:	238.5	Omega-3 (g):	0.13
Protein (g):	16.10	Omega-6 (g):	0.82
Carbohydrates (g):	7.77	Phosphorus (mg):	303.75
Dietary Fiber (g):	1.35	Potassium (mg):	177.48
Fat (g):	16.07	Sodium (mg):	614.65

Preparation

In a bowl, combine the arugula, clementine and Parmesan cheese. Drizzle on the vinegar and oil, season with the pepper, and toss.

Ginger Chicken with Cucumber-Spinach Salad

Prep Time: 1 Hour 20 Minutes
Servings: 5

Ingredients

- **7 chicken breast halves, pounded to ¼ inch thick**
- **2 scallions, trimmed and thinly sliced**
- **1 3-inch piece fresh ginger, peeled and thinly sliced**
- **1 lime, halved**
- **¼ cup olive oil**
- **½ teaspoon kosher salt**
- **¼ teaspoon freshly ground black pepper**
- **2 teaspoons lemon juice**
- **3 cups baby spinach**
- **1 small cucumber, seeded and thinly sliced (about ⅔ cup)**
- **½ small red onion, thinly sliced**
- **1 red chili pepper, seeded and thinly sliced**

Per Serving

Calories:	300.60	**Omega-3 (g):**	0.17
Protein (g):	39.33	**Omega-6 (g):**	1.38
Carbohydrates (g):	5.56	**Phosphorus (mg):**	349.67
Dietary Fiber (g):	1.44	**Potassium (mg):**	635.91
Fat (g):	13.06	**Sodium (mg):**	357.61

Not recommended for pre-dialysis patients on a potassium restriction.

Preparation

In a large bowl, combine the chicken, scallions, half the ginger, the juice from the lime, half the oil, ¼ teaspoon of the salt and half the ground pepper. Toss to combine well, and set aside for 15 minutes. Meanwhile, in a large saucepan, combine the rest of the ginger and the juiced lime halves. Add about an inch of water, place a large steamer basket (or large colander) in the pan, and bring to a boil. Remove the chicken from the marinade, and place in the steamer in a single layer. Steam until cooked through, about 5 minutes, flipping once halfway through. Remove to a plate and cover to keep warm. Reserve 3 cooked chicken breast halves for another use. In a large bowl, whisk together the lemon juice and the remaining oil, salt and pepper. Add the spinach, cucumber, red onion and chili pepper. Toss well. Serve the remaining chicken topped with the Cucumber-Spinach Salad.

Grilled Sweet Potatoes and Scallions

Sides

You didn't think we'd leave your entrees all by their lonesome, did you? These brilliant sides will complement any meal and will leave your kidneys complimenting you for your good behavior.

Apple Glazed Carrots

Prep Time: 45 Minutes

Servings: 4

Pr **Pd** **Tr**

Ingredients

- **2 cups carrots, baby, fresh or frozen**
- **¼ cup apple juice**
- **¼ cup apple jelly**
- **1 ½ teaspoons Dijon mustard**

Per Serving

Calories:	126.42	**Omega-3 (g):**	0.02
Protein (g):	1.25	**Omega-6 (g):**	0.11
Carbohydrates (g):	31.25	**Phosphorus (mg):**	53.63
Dietary Fiber (g):	3.48	**Potassium (mg):**	452.70
Fat (g):	0.31	**Sodium (mg):**	166.02

Not recommended for pre-dialysis patients on a potassium restriction.

Preparation

Place carrots and apple juice in a medium non-stick skillet. Bring to boil. Reduce heat; cover and simmer 7 to 9 minutes or until carrots are crisp-tender. Uncover; cook over medium heat until liquid evaporates. Stir in jelly and mustard; stir and cook over medium heat until jelly melts and carrots are glazed.

Grilled Sweet Potatoes and Scallions

Prep Time: 45 Minutes

Servings: 4

Pr **Pd** **Tr**

Ingredients

- **4 large sweet potatoes, par-cooked and cut into ½-inch slices**
- **8 scallions**
- **¾ cup olive oil, divided**
- **2 tablespoons Dijon mustard**
- **½ cup cider vinegar**
- **¼ cup balsamic vinegar**
- **2 teaspoons honey**
- **Freshly ground pepper**
- **¼ cup coarsely chopped flat-leaf parsley**

Per Serving

Calories:	520.47	**Omega-3 (g):**	0.35
Protein (g):	3.01	**Omega-6 (g):**	3.80
Carbohydrates (g):	38.10	**Phosphorus (mg):**	83.86
Dietary Fiber (g):	5.06	**Potassium (mg):**	595.47
Fat (g):	40.89	**Sodium (mg):**	205.66

Not recommended for pre-dialysis patients on a potassium restriction.

Preparation

Preheat grill to high. Brush sweet potatoes and scallions with ¼ cup of the oil, and arrange on grill. Grill sweet potatoes for 3 to 4 minutes on each side, or until just tender. Grill scallions until softened and marked. Remove scallions from the grill, and cut into thin slices. In a large bowl, whisk together the remaining ½ cup olive oil, the mustard, vinegars and honey. Season with pepper, to taste. Add sweet potatoes, scallions and parsley, and toss until sweet potatoes are well coated. Transfer to a platter, and serve.

Green Beans with Walnut Pesto

Prep Time: 45 Minutes

Servings: 8

Pr Tr

Ingredients

- **1 ½ pounds green beans, trimmed**
- **1 cup walnuts**
- **½ cup olive oil**
- **1 tablespoon lemon juice**
- **½ teaspoon kosher salt**
- **Freshly ground black pepper**

Per Serving

Calories:	242.72	**Omega-3 (g):**	0.45
Protein (g):	5.32	**Omega-6 (g):**	6.43
Carbohydrates (g):	7.75	**Phosphorus (mg):**	112.65
Dietary Fiber (g):	3.97	**Potassium (mg):**	261.49
Fat (g):	22.83	**Sodium (mg):**	151.19

Preparation

In a large pot of boiling water, cook the beans until crisp-tender, about 3 minutes. Drain, and run under cold water to stop the cooking.

Meanwhile, toast the walnuts in a skillet over medium heat until lightly golden, 6 to 7 minutes, stirring occasionally. Reserve half the walnuts, and crush the remainder in a resealable plastic bag with a meat pounder or rolling pin. In a large bowl, whisk together the oil, lemon juice, salt, and a few grinds of pepper. Add the crushed walnuts, whole walnuts and beans, and toss to coat well. Serve cold or at room temperature. (Can be made up to 1 day ahead. Cover and refrigerate.)

Mushroom and Onion Sauté

Prep Time: 45 Minutes

Servings: 4

Pr Pd Tr

Ingredients

- **1 large onion**
- **2 tablespoons olive oil**
- **1 pound fresh mushrooms**
- **⅛ cup dry Sherry (or your preference)**

Per Serving

Calories:	111.58	**Omega-3 (g):**	0.06
Protein (g):	3.89	**Omega-6 (g):**	0.77
Carbohydrates (g):	8.33	**Phosphorus (mg):**	107.18
Dietary Fiber (g):	1.89	**Potassium (mg):**	416.93
Fat (g):	7.17	**Sodium (mg):**	6.53

Not recommended for pre-dialysis patients on a potassium restriction.

Preparation

Cut onion into slices. Heat oil in sauté pan. Sauté onion slices until transparent and slightly browned. Cut mushrooms in slices, including stems. Add to onions. Add sherry. Mix and cover – simmer for 15 minutes, stirring occasionally.

Broiled Tomatoes

Prep Time: 45 Minutes

Servings: 6

Pr Pd Tr

Ingredients

- **3 large salad tomatoes**
- **3 large garlic cloves, cut lengthwise into slivers**
- **2 tablespoons fresh rosemary or 2 teaspoons dried rosemary leaves**
- **½ teaspoon kosher salt**
- **Freshly ground black pepper**
- **¼ cup olive oil**

Per Serving

Calories:	98.96	Omega-3 (g):	0.07
Protein (g):	0.92	Omega-6 (g):	0.91
Carbohydrates (g):	4.19	Phosphorus (mg):	24.54
Dietary Fiber (g):	1.21	Potassium (mg):	225.81
Fat (g):	9.22	Sodium (mg):	199.02

Preparation

Heat broiler to 500° F. Cut the tomatoes crosswise in half, and place them, cut-side up, on a broiling pan or shallow baking pan. Stick the garlic slivers into the tomatoes. Sprinkle with the rosemary, salt and a few grinds of pepper. Drizzle with the oil. Broil about 3 inches from the heat for 10 to 15 minutes or just until the tomatoes release their juices and the garlic begins to brown. Spoon the pan juices over the tomatoes before serving. Serve as a side dish for breakfast, lunch or dinner. Unlike roasted tomatoes, broiled, grilled and pan-broiled tomatoes get sweeter and maintain their shape because the cooking is so brief.

Mashed Tomato Potatoes

Prep Time: 1 Hour

Servings: 8

Pr Pd Tr

Ingredients

- **2 pounds Yukon Gold potatoes (about 6), peeled and cut into 2-inch pieces**
- **2 garlic cloves, peeled**
- **½ cup milk**
- **¼ cup (½ stick) unsalted butter**
- **¼ cup chopped flat-leaf parsley**
- **3 scallions, trimmed and chopped**
- **½ cup grated Parmesan cheese**
- **½ teaspoon kosher salt**
- **2 pounds salad tomatoes (about 5 medium), chopped**

Per Serving

Calories:	206.27	Omega-3 (g):	0.06
Protein (g):	5.58	Omega-6 (g):	0.30
Carbohydrates (g):	29.63	Phosphorus (mg):	128.91
Dietary Fiber (g):	3.51	Potassium (mg):	682.40
Fat (g):	8.17	Sodium (mg):	246.62

Not recommended for pre-dialysis patients on a potassium restriction.

Preparation

Place the potatoes and garlic in a large saucepan and cover with water. Bring to a boil; cover and simmer about 20 minutes or until a fork easily pierces a potato. Drain the potatoes and garlic. Mash with a potato masher or a fork until smooth. Blend in the milk, butter, parsley, scallions, Parmesan cheese and salt. Gently fold in the tomatoes.

Grilled Asparagus with Mozzarella
Prep Time: 20 Minutes
Servings: 4

Pr Pd Tr

Ingredients

- **4 tablespoons fresh lemon juice**
- **¼ cup olive oil**
- **1 small shallot, finely chopped**
- **1 tablespoon finely chopped parsley**
- **1 teaspoon finely chopped oregano**
- **20 large asparagus stalks, peeled**
- **Freshly ground pepper to taste**
- **Olive oil for brushing cheese**
- **¼ pound fresh mozzarella, cut into four ½-inch-thick slices**

Per Serving

Calories:	219.93	**Omega-3 (g):**	0.17
Protein (g):	9.32	**Omega-6 (g):**	1.38
Carbohydrates (g):	7.06	**Phosphorus (mg):**	188.27
Dietary Fiber (g):	2.31	**Potassium (mg):**	271.98
Fat (g):	18.17	**Sodium (mg):**	217.98

Preparation

Preheat grill. In a bowl, mix together lemon juice, ¼ cup olive oil, shallot, parsley, and oregano. Brush asparagus with olive oil, and season with pepper to taste. Grill for 3 to 4 minutes or until just tender. Divide the asparagus among 4 plates, and immediately top with a slice of the cheese. Drizzle with lemon juice mixture.

Broccoli, Sweet Potatoes, and Pears
Prep Time: 45 Minutes
Servings: 4

Pr He Pd Tr

Ingredients

- **1 small stalk broccoli, cut into pieces (about ½ cup)**
- **1 sweet potato, scrubbed and cut into 1-inch chunks**
- **2 tablespoons olive oil**
- **1 tablespoon water**
- **1 pear, unpeeled, cut into 2-inch chunks**
- **¼ teaspoon kosher salt**
- **Freshly ground black pepper**

Per Serving

Calories:	115.49	**Omega-3 (g):**	0.06
Protein (g):	0.98	**Omega-6 (g):**	0.64
Carbohydrates (g):	13.70	**Phosphorus (mg):**	27.14
Dietary Fiber (g):	2.55	**Potassium (mg):**	194.08
Fat (g):	6.86	**Sodium (mg):**	167.55

Preparation

Preheat oven to 500° F. Toss the broccoli and sweet potato with the oil and water in a shallow roasting pan. Place in the oven, and roast 20 minutes, turning occasionally, until browned. Add the pear, and roast until the vegetables are tender, about 10 minutes more. Remove from oven, and toss with the salt and pepper.

Butternut Squash with Cumin Couscous

Prep Time: 1 Hour 30 Minutes
Servings: 8

Ingredients

- **1 butternut squash (2 pounds)**
- **2 tablespoons olive oil**
- **1 large yellow onion, diced**
- **2 cloves garlic, finely chopped**
- **¼ teaspoon cayenne**
- **⅛ teaspoon ground cinnamon**
- **⅛ teaspoon ground nutmeg**
- **1 teaspoon ground cumin**
- **1 cup canned diced tomatoes**
- **⅓ cup dark or golden raisins**
- **1 32-ounce container low-sodium vegetable broth**
- **1 15.5-ounce can chickpeas, rinsed and drained**
- **1 teaspoon kosher salt**
- **1 ½ cups water**
- **1 ½ cups couscous**
- **2 tablespoons chopped fresh flat-leaf parsley leaves**
- **¼ cup (1 ounce) almonds, chopped**

Per Serving

Calories:	248.68	**Omega-3 (g):**	0.04
Protein (g):	8.61	**Omega-6 (g):**	0.92
Carbohydrates (g):	42.44	**Phosphorus (mg):**	159.33
Dietary Fiber (g):	4.30	**Potassium (mg):**	724.21
Fat (g):	6.73	**Sodium (mg):**	568.30

Not recommended for Pre-Diaysis patients on a potassium restriction.

Preparation

Halve and peel the squash. Remove the seeds, and cut the squash into 1-inch chunks. Heat the oil in a Dutch oven over medium heat. Add the onion and cook for 5 minutes. Add the garlic, cayenne, cinnamon, nutmeg and ½ teaspoon of the cumin, and cook for 1 minute. Stir in the squash, tomatoes, raisins, broth, chickpeas and ½ teaspoon of the salt. Bring to a boil. Reduce heat, cover, and simmer for 10 minutes. Uncover and cook until the squash is tender, 15 to 20 minutes. Meanwhile, in a medium saucepan, bring 1 ½ cups water and the remaining cumin and salt to a boil. Stir in the couscous. Cover, remove from heat, and let stand for 5 to 10 minutes. Fluff with a fork. Divide the couscous among individual bowls, and ladle the squash mixture over the top. Sprinkle with the parsley and almonds.

Curried Rice

Prep Time: 20 Minutes
Servings: 4

Ingredients

- **2 cups hot steamed rice**
- **1 egg yolk, slightly beaten***
- **½ teaspoon curry powder**
- **Cayenne to taste**

Preparation

Mix ingredients lightly.

Per Serving

Calories:	117.91	**Omega-3 (g):**	0.02
Protein (g):	2.86	**Omega-6 (g):**	0.24
Carbohydrates (g):	22.68	**Phosphorus (mg):**	52.08
Dietary Fiber (g):	0.46	**Potassium (mg):**	40.67
Fat (g):	1.42	**Sodium (mg):**	3.03

*People with compromised immune systems and children should not eat raw eggs or items containing raw eggs because they may contain Salmonella.

Asparagus Sesame Salad
Prep Time: 45 Minutes
Servings: 4

Pr Pd Tr

Ingredients

- **1 pound asparagus**
- **¼ cup rice vinegar**
- **2 tablespoons soy sauce**
- **1 tablespoon roasted sesame oil**
- **2 tablespoons chopped fresh cilantro**
- **⅛ teaspoon coarse salt**
- **1 ½ cups baby arugula or mesclun salad**
- **2 tablespoons sesame seeds**

Per Serving

Calories:	83.81	**Omega-3 (g):**	0.05
Protein (g):	3.71	**Omega-6 (g):**	2.40
Carbohydrates (g):	6.76	**Phosphorus (mg):**	102.52
Dietary Fiber (g):	3.07	**Potassium (mg):**	291.57
Fat (g):	5.79	**Sodium (mg):**	295.96

Preparation

Heat a large pan of lightly salted water to boiling over high heat. Peel the asparagus stalks, and trim the ends. Cut the stalks diagonally into 1-inch pieces. Blanch in boiling water 3 minutes or until bright green. Drain in a colander and rinse under cold water to stop the cooking. In a large bowl, combine the vinegar, soy sauce, sesame oil, cilantro and salt. Add the asparagus, and toss until well combined. To serve, pile some salad greens on each of 4 plates. Spoon the dressed asparagus onto the greens, and sprinkle with sesame seeds.

Noodles Romano
Prep Time: 45 Minutes
Servings: 6

Pr Tr

Ingredients

- **½ cup margarine**
- **2 tablespoons dried parsley**
- **1 teaspoon dried basil**
- **6 ounces light cream cheese**
- **⅛ teaspoon pepper**
- **8 ounces spaghetti**
- **1 garlic clove**
- **¾ cup Parmesan cheese**

Per Serving

Calories:	387.25	**Omega-3 (g):**	0.19
Protein (g):	12.01	**Omega-6 (g):**	4.90
Carbohydrates (g):	31.43	**Phosphorus (mg):**	178.66
Dietary Fiber (g):	1.12	**Potassium (mg):**	151.30
Fat (g):	23.64	**Sodium (mg):**	418.61

Preparation

Combine ¼ cup margarine, parsley flakes and basil. Blend cream cheese and pepper. Stir in ⅔ cup boiling water. Blend mixture well. Keep warm over pan of hot water. Cook noodles in unsalted water until just tender; drain. Cook minced garlic in ¼ cup unsalted margarine for 1 to 2 minutes then pour over noodles, tossing lightly and quickly to coat well. Sprinkle with ½ cup Parmesan cheese; toss again. Pile noodles on warm serving platter. Spoon warm cream cheese sauce over noodles. Sprinkle with remaining ¼ cup Parmesan cheese. Garnish with additional parsley.

Green Tea Rice

Prep Time: 45 Minutes
Servings: 2

Ingredients

- **2 teaspoons loose Sencha or Bancha tea, or the tea from 2 green tea bags**
- **½ cup white rice**
- **1 cup water**
- **1 tablespoon sugar**
- **1 tablespoon rice vinegar**
- **¼ teaspoon kosher salt**

Per Serving

Calories:	117.01	Omega-3 (g):	0.00
Protein (g):	1.90	Omega-6 (g):	0.02
Carbohydrates (g):	26.93	Phosphorus (mg):	19.24
Dietary Fiber (g):	0.41	Potassium (mg):	51.91
Fat (g):	0.07	Sodium (mg):	295.48

Preparation

Boil the tea, rice and water in a small saucepan. Reduce heat to low; cover and simmer 20 minutes over low heat or until all the water is absorbed. Remove from heat. Meanwhile, in a small saucepan, over low heat, stir the sugar, vinegar and salt until dissolved. Fold into the cooked rice, and serve.

Lemon-Parsley Risotto

Prep Time: 50 Minutes
Servings: 8

Ingredients

- **3 tablespoons unsalted butter**
- **1 small yellow onion, finely chopped**
- **2 cups Arborio rice**
- **1 cup dry white wine**
- **4 cups low-sodium chicken broth**
- **1 tablespoon fresh lemon juice**
- **¼ teaspoon black pepper**
- **1 cup (4 ounces) grated Parmesan cheese**
- **Zest of 1 lemon, grated**
- **½ cup fresh flat-leaf parsley leaves, chopped**

Per Serving

Calories:	291.63	Omega-3 (g):	0.04
Protein (g):	9.05	Omega-6 (g):	0.25
Carbohydrates (g):	41.35	Phosphorus (mg):	157.53
Dietary Fiber (g):	1.11	Potassium (mg):	220.55
Fat (g):	7.60	Sodium (mg):	435.18

Preparation

Melt 2 tablespoons of the butter in a large skillet over medium heat. Add the onion, and cook for 3 minutes. Add the rice, and cook, stirring constantly, for 2 minutes. Reduce heat, add the wine, and cook, stirring frequently, until the liquid is absorbed. Add the broth, ½ cup at a time, stirring occasionally and waiting until it's absorbed before adding more. This should take about 30 minutes total. The rice should be tender but still slightly firm. Remove from heat. Add the lemon juice, pepper, Parmesan and the remaining butter, and stir until the butter melts. Spoon into individual bowls, and sprinkle with the zest and parsley.

French Green Beans in Garlic

Prep Time: 20 Minutes
Servings: 4

Pr He Pd Tr

Ingredients

- **3 garlic cloves, minced**
- **2 tablespoons olive oil**
- **1 9-ounce package frozen French style green beans**
- **¼ teaspoon basil**

Per Serving

Calories:	84.13	Omega-3 (g):	0.10
Protein (g):	1.29	Omega-6 (g):	0.65
Carbohydrates (g):	5.59	Phosphorus (mg):	23.93
Dietary Fiber (g):	1.84	Potassium (mg):	128.20
Fat (g):	6.90	Sodium (mg):	2.50

Preparation

Sauté garlic in olive oil. Add frozen green beans and basil. Cook for 4 to 5 minutes. Serve crisp.

Carrot, Cabbage and Apple Slaw with Cumin Lime Dressing

Prep Time: 40 Minutes
Servings: 7

Pr Pd Tr

Ingredients

- **1 Granny Smith apple**
- **3 tablespoons fresh lime (or lemon) juice**
- **6 cups (1 ½ [10-ounce] packages) shredded carrots**
- **3 cups shredded purple cabbage (¾ [10-ounce] package)**
- **3 tablespoons extra-virgin olive oil**
- **1 tablespoon finely minced shallot**
- **1 teaspoon salt**
- **¼ teaspoon ground cumin**
- **Freshly ground pepper to taste**
- **2 tablespoons minced fresh mint or parsley leaves**
- **2 tablespoons salted sunflower seed kernels**

Per Serving

Calories:	133.29	Omega-3 (g):	0.07
Protein (g):	2.01	Omega-6 (g):	1.31
Carbohydrates (g):	17.39	Phosphorus (mg):	82.66
Dietary Fiber (g):	3.93	Potassium (mg):	445.64
Fat (g):	7.23	Sodium (mg):	383.71

Not recommended for pre-dialysis patients on a potassium restriction.

Preparation

Core and slice the apple; toss in 1 tablespoon of the lime juice. Place carrots and cabbage in a large bowl, and cover with boiling water. Let sit 5 minutes; drain and cool slightly. Whisk together oil, shallot, the remaining lime juice, salt and cumin; add freshly ground pepper to taste. Toss carrots, cabbage and apple in a large bowl with dressing, mint and sunflower seeds. Serve at room temperature or chilled.

Creamed Spinach Gratin

Prep Time: 55 Minutes
Servings: 8

Ingredients

- 1 clove garlic, halved
- 2 tablespoons unsalted butter, plus more for the dish
- 5 shallots, thinly sliced crosswise
- 5 10-ounce boxes frozen spinach, thawed
- 8 ounces cream cheese, at room temperature
- 1 cup heavy cream
- 1 cup whole milk
- 1 cup grated Gruyère or Swiss cheese
- ½ teaspoon black pepper
- 1 teaspoon ground nutmeg

Per Serving

Calories:	362.06	Omega-3 (g):	0.68
Protein (g):	14.70	Omega-6 (g):	0.69
Carbohydrates (g):	13.41	Phosphorus (mg):	252.92
Dietary Fiber (g):	5.60	Potassium (mg):	808.98
Fat (g):	30.05	Sodium (mg):	557.27

Not recommended for pre-dialysis patients on a potassium restriction.

Preparation

Preheat oven to 375° F. Rub the sides and bottom of a buttered 8-inch baking dish with the garlic; discard garlic. In a skillet, over medium heat, melt the butter. Add the shallots, and cook until softened, 5 to 7 minutes. Squeeze the spinach to remove any excess liquid. In a large bowl, combine the spinach, cream cheese, heavy cream, milk, Gruyère or Swiss cheese, pepper, nutmeg and shallots. Transfer to the buttered baking dish. Bake, uncovered, until bubbling and lightly golden, about 25 minutes.

Make ahead: Assemble the gratin in advance, and refrigerate it overnight. Allow an extra 30 minutes of baking time.

Lemony Sugar Snap Peas with Avocado

Prep Time: 15 Minutes
Servings: 4

Ingredients

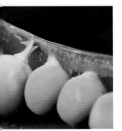

- ½ teaspoon Dijon mustard
- 1 tablespoon lemon juice
- 1 tablespoon olive oil
- ¼ teaspoon kosher salt
- ⅛ teaspoon freshly ground pepper
- ¼ pound raw sugar snap peas
- 1 peeled and sliced Hass avocado

Per Serving

Calories:	123.58	Omega-3 (g):	0.09
Protein (g):	1.85	Omega-6 (g):	1.16
Carbohydrates (g):	6.67	Phosphorus (mg):	41.58
Dietary Fiber (g):	4.30	Potassium (mg):	303.41
Fat (g):	10.86	Sodium (mg):	157.45

Preparation

In a bowl, whisk together Dijon mustard, lemon juice, olive oil, kosher salt and freshly ground pepper. Add raw sugar snap peas and avocado, tossing gently to combine.

Couscous and Feta-Stuffed Peppers
Prep Time: 1 Hour 30 Minutes
Servings: 4

Pr Pd Tr

Ingredients

- **Vegetable-oil cooking spray**
- **1 ¼ cups low-sodium chicken or vegetable broth**
- **⅔ cup couscous**
- **4 large bell peppers, mixed colors**
- **2 teaspoons olive oil**
- **½ cup chopped onion**
- **6 ounces zucchini, quartered lengthwise, then sliced across thinly**
- **6 ounces yellow squash, quartered lengthwise, then sliced across thinly**
- **½ teaspoon fennel seeds**
- **½ teaspoon dried oregano**
- **1 cup cherry tomatoes, cut in half**
- **15 ounces canned chickpeas, drained and rinsed**
- **4 ounces crumbled feta cheese (about 1 cup)**

Per Serving

Calories:	422.13	**Omega-3 (g):**	0.19
Protein (g):	18.31	**Omega-6 (g):**	0.48
Carbohydrates (g):	62.41	**Phosphorus (mg):**	365.7
Dietary Fiber (g):	10.77	**Potassium (mg):**	452.65
Fat (g):	12.21	**Sodium (mg):**	416.32

Not recommended for pre-dialysis patients on a potassium restriction.

Preparation

Preheat oven to 350°F. Coat a small baking dish with cooking spray. Bring the broth to a boil in a saucepan, add the couscous, cover the pan, and remove it from the heat. Meanwhile, bring a large pot of water to a boil. Cut the stems and top half inch off the bell peppers, and scoop out the seeds and membranes. Boil trimmed peppers for 5 minutes then drain them upside down. Heat oil in a nonstick skillet. Add onion, zucchini, yellow squash, fennel seeds and oregano. Cook, stirring frequently, for 5 minutes or until vegetables are softened. Remove from heat, and stir in the tomatoes and chickpeas. Using a fork, scrape the couscous into the skillet, and toss with the vegetables. Stir in the crumbled feta. Place peppers upright in the baking dish, and fill them with couscous. Bake 15 minutes. Serve immediately.

Rosemary Sage Burgers with Apple Slaw and Chive "Mayo"

Entrees

Eating healthy and staying
KidneyWise™ doesn't have to be
hard. Our entrees are easy, they're
delicious, and we think they're
pretty good to look at, too. And
we're not even bragging. OK,
maybe a little bit.

Spicy Chicken

Prep Time: 1 Hour
Servings: 4

Ingredients

- 2 tablespoons balsamic vinegar or red wine vinegar
- 1 tablespoon olive oil
- ½ teaspoon dried rosemary, crushed
- ¼ teaspoon ground cumin
- ⅛ teaspoon ground coriander
- ⅛ teaspoon black pepper
- Dash of ground red pepper
- 8 small green onions, cut into 2-inch pieces and/or 4 small purple boiling onions, cut into wedges
- 4 medium skinless, boneless chicken breast halves (about 1 pound total)
- 2 cups hot cooked rice
- 2 tablespoons peach or apricot preserves, melted (optional)

Per Serving

Calories:	314.25	Omega-3 (g):	0.09
Protein (g):	30.36	Omega-6 (g):	0.70
Carbohydrates (g):	33.83	Phosphorus (mg):	281.66
Dietary Fiber (g):	2.65	Potassium (mg):	56.34
Fat (g):	5.30	Sodium (mg):	83.49

Preparation

In a small bowl, combine vinegar, olive oil, rosemary, cumin, coriander, black pepper and red pepper. Thread onions on eight 6-inch skewers. Set aside. Grill the chicken on the rack of an uncovered grill directly over medium heat for 12 to 15 minutes or until chicken is tender and no longer pink, turning and brushing once with the vinegar mixture. Place kabobs on grill rack next to chicken the last 5 minutes of grilling, turning and brushing once with vinegar mixture. Serve chicken and kabobs over rice. If desired, drizzle with preserves.

Honey Garlic Pork Chops

Prep Time: 4 Hours 30 Minutes (includes marinating time)
Servings: 4

Ingredients

- ¼ cup lemon juice
- ¼ cup honey
- 2 tablespoons soy sauce
- 1 tablespoon dry sherry
- 2 minced garlic cloves
- 4 boneless center-cut pork chops

Per Serving

Calories:	224.92	Omega-3 (g):	0.01
Protein (g):	22.81	Omega-6 (g):	0.42
Carbohydrates (g):	19.87	Phosphorus (mg):	191.62
Dietary Fiber (g):	0.18	Potassium (mg):	298.02
Fat (g):	6.04	Sodium (mg):	290.34

Preparation

Combine all ingredients except pork chops in small bowl. Place pork in shallow baking dish; pour marinade over pork. Cover and refrigerate 4 hours or overnight. Remove pork from marinade. Preheat the boiler. Heat remaining marinade in small saucepan over medium heat to simmer. Broil pork 4 to 6 inches from heat source 12 to 15 minutes, turning once during cooking and basting frequently with marinade. Also great grilled!

Rosemary Sage Burgers with Apple Slaw and Chive "Mayo"
Prep Time: 45 Minutes
Servings: 4

Pr **Pd** **Tr**

Ingredients

Burgers
- ½ pound extra-lean ground round beef
- ½ pound lean ground pork
- 1 tablespoon chopped fresh rosemary
- 1 tablespoon chopped fresh sage
- ¼ teaspoon salt
- 4 whole-grain buns
- 1 cup baby spinach leaves

Chive "Mayo"
- ½ cup nonfat sour cream
- 2 tablespoons chopped fresh chives
- 1 dash each salt and pepper

Apple Slaw
- 3 green apples, peeled, cored and grated
- 2 teaspoons extra-virgin olive oil
- 1 teaspoon fresh lemon juice

Per Serving

Calories:	432.82	**Omega-3 (g):**	0.11
Protein (g):	26.93	**Omega-6 (g):**	2.24
Carbohydrates (g):	39.50	**Phosphorus (mg):**	350.7
Dietary Fiber (g):	4.95	**Potassium (mg):**	655.27
Fat (g):	19.37	**Sodium (mg):**	505.01

Not recommended for pre-dialysis patients on a potassium restriction.

Preparation

Preheat grill to medium high. Combine beef, pork, rosemary, sage and salt in a medium-sized bowl; form into 4 patties. In a small bowl, combine mayo ingredients. In a medium-sized bowl, combine slaw ingredients. Grill patties 4 minutes on each side or until juices run clear. Toast the buns, and spread each top with chive "mayo". Place burger on bun, and top with slaw and several spinach leaves.

Grilled Salmon with Papaya-Mint Salsa

Grilled Salmon with Papaya-Mint Salsa

Prep Time: 40 Minutes
Servings: 4

Ingredients

- ¼ cup peeled and chopped papaya
- ¼ cup chopped yellow bell pepper
- ¼ cup thinly sliced green onion
- 1 tablespoon chopped pimiento
- 1 tablespoon chopped fresh mint
- 1 tablespoon rice wine vinegar or white vinegar
- 1 tablespoon fresh lime juice
- 1 teaspoon grated fresh ginger
- 1 teaspoon seeded and minced jalapeño pepper
- Vegetable-oil cooking spray
- 4 salmon steaks (5 ounces each) or fillets, about 1 to 1 ¼ inches thick
- Pepper to taste

Per Serving

Calories:	277.25	Omega-3 (g):	2.84
Protein (g):	28.65	Omega-6 (g):	2.47
Carbohydrates (g):	3.35	Phosphorus (mg):	339.45
Dietary Fiber (g):	0.65	Potassium (mg):	611.01
Fat (g):	15.45	Sodium (mg):	84.90

Not recommended for pre-dialysis patients on a potassium restriction.

Preparation

For salsa, combine all ingredients except the salmon in a small bowl. Cover and chill at least 30 minutes. Lightly coat grill or broiler pan with cooking spray. Sprinkle both sides of fish with pepper. Grill or broil fish 5 minutes on each side or until done. Top each steak with ¼ cup salsa and serve with whole-wheat couscous, if desired.

Filet with Pesto

Prep Time: 45 Minutes
Servings: 4 or 5

Ingredients

- 2 pounds center cut fillet of beef, spiral cut
- Freshly ground pepper
- ½ cup store-bought pesto
- Extra-virgin olive oil
- 8 long wooden skewers, soaked in cold water for at least 30 minutes.

Per Serving

Calories:	693.29	Omega-3 (g):	0.46
Protein (g):	49.33	Omega-6 (g):	3.03
Carbohydrates (g):	0.63	Phosphorus (mg):	398.85
Dietary Fiber (g):	0.09	Potassium (mg):	613.41
Fat (g):	53.82	Sodium (mg):	261.03

Not recommended for pre-dialysis patients on a potassium restriction.

Preparation

With the heel of your hand or a meat mallet, pound the meat and flatten to a thickness of about ½ inch. Sprinkle the inside of the meat with pepper. Spread the pesto over the meat, leaving a 1-inch border on 1 long side. Roll the meat toward the border.

With your knife, mark the fillet at 1-inch intervals. Run skewers through your fillet in between your knife marks so that each portion has a skewer securing it. Using your knife marks as a guide, cut your fillet into slices. Drizzle with the oil. Preheat the grill or a grill pan. Grill slices over high heat for about 3 to 4 minutes per side for medium rare. Let rest for a few minutes before serving.

Chicken and Spanish Rice

Prep Time: 1 Hour
Servings: 5

Pr Pd Tr

Ingredients

- 1 cup onion, chopped
- ¾ cup green peppers
- 2 teaspoons vegetable oil
- 1 8-ounce can tomato sauce*
- 1 teaspoon parsley, chopped
- ½ teaspoon black pepper
- ¼ teaspoon garlic, minced
- 5 cups cooked brown rice (cooked in unsalted water)
- 3 ½ cups chicken breasts (cooked, skin and bone removed, and diced)

Per Serving

The analyses in bold italic are for the reduced sodium version

Calories:	428.15	*444.48*	Omega-3 (g):	0.11	*0.11*
Protein (g):	36.59	*36.86*	Omega-6 (g):	2.26	*2.27*
Carbohydrates (g):	52.77	*57.61*	Phosphorus (mg):	411.77	*417.57*
Dietary Fiber (g):	5.10	*4.87*	Potassium (mg):	576.87	*585.71*
Fat (g):	7.90	*7.90*	Sodium (mg):	321.94	*207.63*

Preparation

In a large skillet, sauté onion and green peppers in oil for 5 minutes over medium heat. Add tomato sauce and spices. Heat through. Add cooked rice and chicken. Heat through.

* To reduce sodium, use one 4-ounce can of low-sodium tomato sauce and one 4-ounce can of regular tomato sauce.

Tangy Tuna and Sun-Dried Tomato Wrap

Prep Time: 25 Minutes
Servings: 4

Pr Pd Tr

Ingredients

- 2 (6 ounce) cans chunk light tuna in water, drained
- ¼ cup minced sun-dried tomatoes
- 3 tablespoons low-fat mayonnaise
- 2 tablespoons chopped fresh parsley
- Pepper to taste
- 2 teaspoons stone-ground mustard or Dijon mustard
- 4 leaves red leaf lettuce
- 4 small (8-inch) spinach tortillas or whole wheat tortillas

Per Serving

Calories:	285.86	Omega-3 (g):	0.42
Protein (g):	26.60	Omega-6 (g):	1.79
Carbohydrates (g):	29.19	Phosphorus (mg):	221.34
Dietary Fiber (g):	2.36	Potassium (mg):	452.74
Fat (g):	6.58	Sodium (mg):	157.61

Preparation

In a bowl, combine tuna, tomatoes, mayonnaise, and parsley. Add pepper. Spoon ½ teaspoon mustard on each tortilla. Layer lettuce on each tortilla; then add ¼ tuna mixture on each tortilla, spread to within ¼ inch of the edges, and roll.

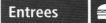

Flank Steak Pinwheels
Prep Time: 1 Hour 30 Minutes
Servings: 4

Ingredients

- ⅔ cup sun-dried tomatoes (not packed in oil)
- 2 cups boiling water
- 1 pound flank steak , trimmed of fat
- 1 clove garlic , minced
- Oil for brushing
- 1 cup baby spinach
- ¼ teaspoon kosher salt
- ½ teaspoon freshly ground pepper
- 8 wooden skewers, soaked in water
- 3 tablespoons light herbed cheese spread, such as Boursin (see variation)

Per Serving

Calories:	203.95	**Omega-3 (g):**	0.08
Protein (g):	26.82	**Omega-6 (g):**	0.30
Carbohydrates (g):	6.23	**Phosphorus (mg):**	277.33
Dietary Fiber (g):	1.36	**Potassium (mg):**	754.71
Fat (g):	7.83	**Sodium (mg):**	427.00

Not recommended for pre-dialysis patients on a potassium restriction.

Preparation

Preheat grill to high. Place sun-dried tomatoes in a bowl; pour boiling water over them, and let steep until softened, about 10 minutes. Drain and chop.

Place steak between 2 large pieces of plastic wrap. Pound each side of the steak thoroughly with the pointed side of a meat mallet until the steak is an even ¼-inch thickness. Rub garlic all over one side of the steak. Spread cheese lengthwise in a 3-inch-wide strip down the middle of the steak. Top with the sun-dried tomatoes and spinach. Starting at one edge of a long side, roll the steak up tightly, tucking in the filling as you go. Carefully rub salt and pepper all over the outside of the steak roll. Turn the roll so the overlapping edge is on top. Push 8 skewers, evenly spaced, through the roll, close to the overlapping edge to hold the roll together. Slice the roll into 8 equal portions, roughly 1 to 1 ½ inches thick, with a skewer in each. Lay the slices on their sides, and push the skewer through so it sticks out about 1 inch.

Oil the grill rack. Grill the pinwheels 3 to 4 minutes per side for medium-rare. Use a spatula when turning them to prevent too much filling from falling out. (Don't worry if the ends of the skewers burn. They will still hold the pinwheels together.) Remove the skewers; let the pinwheels rest for 5 minutes before serving.

Turkey Meatloaf

Prep Time: 45 Minutes
Servings: 5

Ingredients

- **1 pound lean ground turkey**
- **½ cup regular oats, dry**
- **1 large egg, whole**
- **1 tablespoon dehydrated onion flakes**
- **¼ cup low-sodium ketchup**

Per Serving

Calories:	226.53	**Omega-3 (g):**	0.10
Protein (g):	20.00	**Omega-6 (g):**	1.86
Carbohydrates (g):	14.52	**Phosphorus (mg):**	249.92
Dietary Fiber (g):	1.90	**Potassium (mg):**	298 .64
Fat (g):	9.61	**Sodium (mg):**	102.20

Preparation

Preheat oven to 350° F. Combine all ingredients, and mix well. Bake in a loaf pan at 350° F for 25 minutes or to an internal temperature of 165 ° F. Cut into five slices and serve.

Summer Shrimp

Prep Time: 1 Hour
Servings: 4

Ingredients

Marinade
- **2 cloves garlic, smashed**
- **1 tablespoon olive oil**
- **2 teaspoons fresh lime juice**
- **1 teaspoon Worcestershire sauce**
- **1 teaspoon dried oregano**
- **¼ teaspoon freshly ground black pepper**

Shrimp
- **24 large shrimp (about 1 pound), peeled and deveined**
- **1 small red onion**
- **16 serrano chilies**
- **8 bamboo skewers, 10 inches long, soaked in water 30 minutes**

Per Serving

Calories:	116.47	**Omega-3 (g):**	0.25
Protein (g):	10.16	**Omega-6 (g):**	0.42
Carbohydrates (g):	9.88	**Phosphorus (mg):**	129.7
Dietary Fiber (g):	2.54	**Potassium (mg):**	78.25
Fat (g):	2.62	**Sodium (mg):**	54.32

Preparation

In a blender or mini food processor, process all marinade ingredients until smooth. Toss shrimp with marinade in a bowl to coat well. Set aside at least 10 minutes, or up to 2 hours. Cut onion into 8 wedges; then cut each wedge lengthwise into thirds. Thread 1 chili onto each skewer. (If you prefer metal skewers, be sure to spray them first with a vegetable oil cooking spray so shrimp and vegetables don't stick.) Add 1 shrimp, and chunk of onion to each skewer; repeat twice. Finish each skewer with a second chili. Heat a cast-iron grill pan or an electric or gas grill over high heat. Cook skewers, covered, turning once, until shrimp are cooked through and onions are charred and just tender, about 5 minutes per side. (You can use a charcoal grill, but shrimp will cook faster.) Serve with salsa.

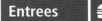

Veal Marsala

Prep Time: 45 Minutes
Servings: 4

Ingredients

- **1 pound veal leg round steak or veal sirloin steak**
- **3 cups fresh mushrooms (such as crimini, porcini, baby portobello or button), quartered, halved or sliced**
- **4 teaspoons olive oil or cooking oil**
- **¼ teaspoon salt**
- **¼ teaspoon black pepper**
- **¾ cup dry Marsala**
- **½ cup sliced green onions (about 4)**
- **1 tablespoon snipped fresh sage or ½ teaspoon dried sage, crushed**
- **1 tablespoon cold water**
- **1 teaspoon cornstarch**
- **⅛ teaspoon salt**
- **Hot cooked noodles (optional)**
- **Fresh herb sprigs (optional)**

Per Serving

Calories:	223.75	Omega-3 (g):	0.06
Protein (g):	25.75	Omega-6 (g):	0.75
Carbohydrates (g):	4.10	Phosphorus (mg):	302.71
Dietary Fiber (g):	1.13	Potassium (mg):	657.45
Fat (g):	8.20	Sodium (mg):	293.65

Not recommended for pre-dialysis patients on a potassium restriction.

Preparation

Cut veal into four serving-sized pieces. Place each veal piece between two pieces of plastic wrap. Use the flat side of a meat mallet to lightly pound each slice to about ⅛-inch-thick, working from center to edges. Remove plastic wrap. Set meat aside. In a 12-inch skillet, cook the mushrooms in 2 teaspoons of the hot oil for 4 to 5 minutes or until tender. Remove from skillet; set aside. Sprinkle meat with the ¼ teaspoon salt and the pepper. In the same skillet, cook veal, half at a time, in the remaining 2 teaspoons hot oil over medium-high heat for 2 to 3 minutes or until no longer pink, turning once. Transfer to dinner plates; keep warm. Add Marsala to drippings in skillet. Bring to boiling. Boil mixture gently, uncovered, for 1 minute, scraping up any browned bits. Return mushrooms to skillet; add green onions and sage. In a small bowl, stir together cold water, cornstarch and the ⅛ teaspoon salt; add to skillet. Cook, and stir until slightly thickened and bubbly; cook, and stir 1 minute more. To serve, spoon the mushroom mixture over meat. Serve immediately. If desired, serve with noodles, and garnish with herb sprigs.

Chicken Salad

Prep Time: 1 Hour
Servings: 5

Ingredients

- **3 ¼ cups chicken breast, cooked, cubed and skinless**
- **¼ cup celery, chopped**
- **1 tablespoon lemon juice**
- **½ teaspoon onion powder**
- **⅛ teaspoon salt**
- **3 tablespoons low-fat mayonnaise**

Per Serving

Calories:	59.74	**Omega-3 (g):**	0.12
Protein (g):	6.67	**Omega-6 (g):**	0.94
Carbohydrates (g):	2.62	**Phosphorus (mg):**	52.76
Dietary Fiber (g):	0.11	**Potassium (mg):**	73.97
Fat (g):	8.25	**Sodium (mg):**	137.99

Preparation

Refrigerate cooked chicken. In a large bowl, combine rest of ingredients, add chilled chicken and mix well.

Shrimp and Crab Gumbo

Prep Time: 1 Hour
Servings: 6

Ingredients

- **4 tablespoons canola oil**
- **6 tablespoons all-purpose flour**
- **1 cup bell pepper, chopped**
- **1 ½ cups onion, diced**
- **1 clove garlic, chopped**
- **1 tablespoon celery leaves or diced celery**
- **4 cups water (divided use)**
- **4 cups low-sodium chicken broth**
- **8 ounces uncooked shrimp**
- **6 ounces crab meat**
- **1 cup green onion tops, diced**
- **¼ cup fresh parsley, chopped**
- **Pepper to taste**
- **1 teaspoon hot sauce (optional)**
- **Hot cooked rice**

Per Serving

Calories:	218.72	**Omega-3 (g):**	0.77
Protein (g):	17.97	**Omega-6 (g):**	1.80
Carbohydrates (g):	13.67	**Phosphorus (mg):**	187.95
Dietary Fiber (g):	1.87	**Potassium (mg):**	493.08
Fat (g):	10.27	**Sodium (mg):**	561.73

Not recommended for pre-dialysis patients on a potassium restriction.

Preparation

To make a roux, heat oil and flour in a large skillet over medium heat. Stir constantly until flour is pecan colored. Add bell pepper, onion, garlic, celery leaves and 1 cup water. Cover and cook on very low heat until vegetables are tender. Increase heat to high, and add 3 cups water and 4 cups low-sodium chicken broth. Boil for 5 minutes. Reduce to medium heat, and add shrimp and crab meat. Boil 10 minutes. Add green onion tops and parsley. Reduce to low heat, and simmer for 5 minutes. Season with pepper and hot sauce. Serve gumbo over hot rice.

Thai Beef Salad

Prep Time: 1 Hour
Servings: 2

Pr Pd Tr

Ingredients

Marinade
- ¼ cup low-sodium soy sauce
- ½ cup honey
- 2 tablespoons fresh orange juice
- 1 tablespoon cilantro
- 1 tablespoon mint leaves
- 1 tablespoon fresh lime juice
- 1 Thai (or serrano) chili
- 2 ½ cloves garlic
- 1 ½-inch piece ginger, peeled and sliced

Salad
- 6 ounces flank steak
- 2 cups Asian vermicelli noodles
- ¼ cup diced tomato
- 2 tablespoons enoki mushrooms (found in Asian markets)
- ⅛ cup thinly sliced red onion
- 10 to 12 grapefruit segments
- 8 cilantro sprigs
- 4 mint sprigs

Dressing
- ¼ cup fresh lime juice
- ¼ cup low-sodium soy sauce
- 2 tablespoons fresh orange juice
- 2 tablespoons dark sesame oil
- 2 ¼ teaspoons fish sauce
- 1 Thai (or serrano) chili, seeded and minced
- 1 ½ cloves garlic
- 1 1-inch piece ginger, peeled and chopped

Per Serving

Calories:	951.31	**Omega-3 (g):**	0.13
Protein (g):	41.79	**Omega-6 (g):**	6.06
Carbohydrates (g):	152.59	**Phosphorus (mg):**	327.75
Dietary Fiber (g):	4.92	**Potassium (mg):**	977.57
Fat (g):	22.11	**Sodium (mg):**	300.22

Not recommended for pre-dialysis patients on a potassium restriction.

Preparation

Mix marinade ingredients in a blender until combined. Pour into a bowl; add steak. Cover with plastic wrap; refrigerate at least 2 hours. Heat grill to medium-high. Cook steak until medium rare, about 2 ½ minutes per side. Cool; slice thin. Cook noodles according to package instructions. Rinse under cold water, place in a bowl, and cover with plastic wrap.

Mix all dressing ingredients in blender until combined. Divide tomato, mushrooms, onion, grapefruit segments, noodles, cilantro and mint between 2 bowls; top with ¼ cup dressing (or mix together, top with ½ cup dressing; then divide). Add steak.

Southwestern Turkey Burger

Prep Time: 45 Minutes

Servings: 4

Ingredients

- **1 egg white, lightly beaten**
- **⅓ cup cheddar cheese, diced**
- **12 ounces lean ground turkey**
- **1 cup kidney beans, drained and rinsed**
- **¼ cup breadcrumbs**
- **⅔ cup chopped onion**
- **⅓ cup chopped fresh cilantro**
- **⅔ cup salsa (plus more for topping)**
- **1 tablespoon canola oil**
- **1 cup green leaf lettuce (about 4 large leaves)**
- **4 English muffins, split and toasted**

Per Serving

Calories:	425.49	Omega-3 (g):	0.42
Protein (g):	27.23	Omega-6 (g):	2.93
Carbohydrates (g):	43.87	Phosphorus (mg):	343.45
Dietary Fiber (g):	5.54	Potassium (mg):	636.44
Fat (g):	15.25	Sodium (mg):	971.02

Preparation

In a large bowl, combine egg white, cheese, turkey, salt, kidney beans, breadcrumbs, onion, cilantro and salsa, and mix thoroughly. Divide the mixture and form into 4 patties. Tuck any pieces of cheese into the burgers with your fingertips to prevent scorching. Heat oil in a large nonstick pan over medium heat. Add burgers and cook 6 to 7 minutes per side or until cooked through. Serve on English muffins, accompanied by lettuce and extra salsa (to use as a topping).

Vegetarian Chili

Tr

Prep Time: 1 Hour 20 Minutes

Servings: 9

Ingredients

- **1 ½ cups sliced celery**
- **1 ½ cups chopped green bell peppers**
- **2 tablespoons olive oil**
- **4 14-½-ounce cans diced tomatoes with onion and garlic**
- **3 15-ounce cans red kidney beans, rinsed and drained**
- **1 15-ounce can Great Northern beans or navy beans, rinsed and drained**
- **1 12-ounce can beer or 1 ½ cups water**
- **1 tablespoon chili powder**
- **1 bay leaf**
- **1 ½ teaspoons dried basil, crushed**
- **1 ½ teaspoons dried oregano, crushed**
- **½ teaspoon pepper**
- **¼ teaspoon bottled hot pepper sauce**
- **Shredded cheddar cheese**

Per Serving

Calories:	264.31	Omega-3 (g):	0.25
Protein (g):	12.24	Omega-6 (g):	0.63
Carbohydrates (g):	40.54	Phosphorus (mg):	246.76
Dietary Fiber (g):	13.58	Potassium (mg):	997.10
Fat (g):	6.16	Sodium (mg):	508.11

Preparation

In a 4-quart Dutch oven, cook celery and green bell peppers in hot oil over medium heat until vegetables are tender, stirring occasionally. Stir in undrained tomatoes, beans, beer or water, chili powder, bay leaf, basil, oregano, pepper and hot pepper sauce. Bring to boiling; reduce heat. Simmer, uncovered, for 1 hour, stirring occasionally. Remove, and discard bay leaf. Serve shredded cheese as a topper.

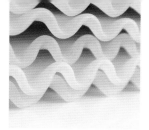

Vegetarian Lasagna
Prep Time: 1 Hour 30 Minutes
Servings: 8

Pr Pd Tr

Ingredients

- **1 pound soft tofu**
- **½ cup grated Parmesan cheese**
- **2 eggs**
- **3 garlic cloves, minced**
- **2 tablespoons each minced fresh basil, thyme and oregano, or 2 teaspoons each dried**
- **⅛ teaspoon freshly ground black pepper**
- **Vegetable oil cooking spray**
- **32 ounces homemade tomato sauce or low-sodium tomato sauce**
- **½ 8-ounce package no-boil lasagna noodles**
- **4 ounces fresh pre-washed baby spinach (2 cups)**
- **8 ounces mozzarella cheese , shredded (2 cups)**

Per Serving

Calories:	205.51	Omega-3 (g):	0.23
Protein (g):	16.57	Omega-6 (g):	1.46
Carbohydrates (g):	15.04	Phosphorus (mg):	285.98
Dietary Fiber (g):	2.23	Potassium (mg):	550.58
Fat (g):	9.77	Sodium (mg):	442.49

Not recommended for pre-dialysis patients on a potassium restriction.

Preparation

Heat oven to 375° F. Combine the tofu, Parmesan cheese, eggs, garlic, herbs, and pepper in a medium bowl. Lightly coat a 13-by-9-inch baking dish with vegetable oil cooking spray. Spread with about 1 cup of the tomato sauce. Arrange one layer of noodles on top. Spread with half the tofu mixture; top with half the spinach, a third of the remaining sauce and a third of the mozzarella. Repeat layers, ending with noodles, sauce and mozzarella. Cover with aluminum foil, and bake 30 to 35 minutes. Let stand 5 minutes before cutting. Recipe can be made ahead to this point. Cool, cover, and refrigerate up to one day ahead. Reheat at 325° F for 20 minutes or until a knife inserted in the center comes out hot.

Teriyaki Wraps

Prep Time: 1 Hour 15 Minutes
Servings: 4

Pd **Tr**

Ingredients

- **2 cups water**
- **1 cup uncooked long grain white rice**
- **2 tablespoons olive oil**
- **1 onion, chopped**
- **1 red bell pepper, chopped**
- **1 small zucchini, chopped**
- **1 small yellow squash, chopped**
- **½ cups low-sodium teriyaki sauce**
- **2 teaspoons garlic powder**
- **1 teaspoon ground black pepper**
- **4 (10-inch) whole wheat tortillas**

Per Serving

Calories:	473.88	Omega-3 (g):	0.15
Protein (g):	14.60	Omega-6 (g):	1.76
Carbohydrates (g):	76.59	Phosphorus (mg):	256.42
Dietary Fiber (g):	4.53	Potassium (mg):	551.28
Fat (g):	12.52	Sodium (mg):	920.39

Preparation

In a saucepan, bring 2 cups water to a boil; add rice. Reduce heat, cover, and simmer for 20 minutes. Heat olive oil in a large skillet over medium heat. Sauté onion, bell pepper, zucchini and yellow squash until onions are tender. Stir in the teriyaki sauce. When the vegetables are tender, stir in the cooked rice, garlic powder, and pepper. Simmer for 3 to 5 minutes. Place ¼ of the rice and vegetables in each tortilla, and roll up.

Vegetarian Spaghetti Sauce

Prep Time: 1 Hour
Servings: 6

Pr **Pd** **Tr**

Ingredients

- **2 tablespoons olive oil**
- **2 small onions, chopped**
- **3 cloves garlic, chopped**
- **1 ¼ cups zucchini, sliced**
- **1 tablespoon oregano, dried**
- **1 tablespoon basil, dried**
- **1 8-ounce can of tomato sauce**
- **2 medium tomatoes, chopped**
- **1 cup water**
- **1 6-ounce can of reduced-sodium tomato paste**
- **Hot cooked spaghetti**

Per Serving

Calories:	99.27	Omega-3 (g):	0.10
Protein (g):	2.71	Omega-6 (g):	0.54
Carbohydrates (g):	13.63	Phosphorus (mg):	61.32
Dietary Fiber (g):	3.40	Potassium (mg):	603.5
Fat (g):	4.94	Sodium (mg):	231.49

Not recommended for pre-dialysis patients on a potassium restriction.

Preparation

In a medium skillet, heat oil. Sauté onions, garlic and zucchini in skillet for 5 minutes on medium heat. Add remaining ingredients and simmer, covered, for 45 minutes. Serve over spaghetti.

Grilled Pork Tenderloin

Prep Time: 1 Hour
Servings: 4

Pr He Pd Tr

Ingredients

Marinade
- **2 oranges, juiced**
- **1 lime, juiced**
- **1 tablespoon Dijon mustard**
- **1 teaspoon ground ginger**
- **1 clove garlic, crushed**
- **1 tablespoon chopped scallions**

Tenderloin
- **1 pork tenderloin (about 12 ounces)**
- **Olive oil for brushing**

Per Serving

Calories:	237.86	**Omega-3 (g):**	0.04
Protein (g):	21.66	**Omega-6 (g):**	0.79
Carbohydrates (g):	19.72	**Phosphorus (mg):**	217.87
Dietary Fiber (g):	1.04	**Potassium (mg):**	167.63
Fat (g):	8.31	**Sodium (mg):**	68.00

Preparation

Combine marinade ingredients in measuring cup, and stir to combine. Place the pork tenderloin in a plastic, sealable bag. Pour marinade over the tenderloin, and seal bag. Marinate overnight in the refrigerator. Preheat an outdoor grill or oven to 350° F. Remove pork tenderloin from marinade, and pat dry. Brush olive oil onto grill and over meat for extra flavor. Reserve marinade. Grill tenderloin until cooked through, about 30 minutes to 40 minutes over medium heat, or roast in oven for 35 to 45 minutes. Allow meat to rest about 10 minutes before cutting into 2-inch serving pieces. While meat is grilling, bring reserved marinade to a boil in a small saucepan; then lower the heat, and gently simmer until it is reduced to about 2 tablespoons. Stir occasionally. Drizzle a small amount of marinade over each piece of meat.

Apricot-Cherry
Trifle

Desserts

No, we aren't kidding. This section includes 20 great desserts that can satisfy both your stomach and your conscience. S'mores, tarts, parfaits, pie and cake. We have them all. And so can you.

Blueberry Tartlets

Prep Time: 3 Hours
Servings: 4

Ingredients

- **2 cups fresh blueberries**
- **2 teaspoons fresh orange juice**
- **1 teaspoon fresh lemon juice**
- **¼ teaspoon vanilla extract**
- **4 teaspoons brown sugar**
- **½ teaspoon grated orange zest, plus extra julienned for garnish**
- **Canola oil cooking spray**
- **⅔ cup raw almonds**
- **½ (packed) cup pitted dates**
- **1 teaspoon water**

Per Serving

Calories:	271.58	Omega-3 (g):	0.06
Protein (g):	6.38	Omega-6 (g):	3.00
Carbohydrates (g):	39.36	Phosphorus (mg):	140.07
Dietary Fiber (g):	7.04	Potassium (mg):	414.89
Fat (g):	12.49	Sodium (mg):	2.93

Preparation

Combine first 6 ingredients in a bowl, cover, and refrigerate. Coat a mixing bowl with cooking spray. Pulse almonds in a food processor until they resemble breadcrumbs. Empty into prepared bowl. Pulse dates with 1 teaspoon water in food processor until well chopped (they will be a little clumpy). Mix with almonds to form a paste. Divide mixture evenly into 4 golf ball-sized rounds. Place each ball between 2 pieces of wax paper, and press to form a 4-inch crust. Turn up edges if desired. Refrigerate 2 hours. Use a spatula to move crusts to serving plates; fill each with ½ cup berries, and drizzle each with some leftover juices from bowl. Top with julienned orange zest.

Strawberry-Mango Parfaits with Ginger Topping

Prep Time: 20 Minutes
Servings: 4

Ingredients

- **1 pint strawberries, stemmed and sliced**
- **2 tablespoons granulated sugar, or to taste**
- **2 tablespoons orange juice**
- **2 teaspoons grated orange rind**
- **1 pint mango sorbet or orange sorbet**
- **1 pint strawberry ice cream**
- **½ cup gingersnap crumbs**
- **2 tablespoons coarsely chopped crystallized ginger (optional)**

Per Serving

Calories:	268.91	Omega-3 (g):	0.07
Protein (g):	3.42	Omega-6 (g):	0.20
Carbohydrates (g):	51.01	Phosphorus (mg):	98.76
Dietary Fiber (g):	2.99	Potassium (mg):	347.7
Fat (g):	6.68	Sodium (mg):	92.91

Preparation

Toss strawberries, sugar, juice and rind in a bowl, and set aside. Place scoops of sorbet and ice cream in deep bowls or parfait glasses. Top with a layer of the strawberry mixture, and repeat with another layer of sorbet and ice cream. Top with the remaining strawberry mixture, crumbs and ginger.

Low-Protein / High-Calorie Smoothie

Prep Time: 15 Minutes
Servings 1

Ingredients

- ¾ cup rice ice cream (Rice Dream™ from Imagine Foods™)
- 1 tablespoon whey protein powder (optional)
- 1 tablespoon olive oil, canola oil coconut oil or flax oil
- ½ cup berries of choice

Per Serving

Calories:	260.58	**Omega-3 (g):**	0.05
Protein (g):	4.62	**Omega-6 (g):**	0.53
Carbohydrates (g):	26.67	**Phosphorus (mg):**	113.97
Dietary Fiber (g):	1.52	**Potassium (mg):**	209.73
Fat (g):	15.62	**Sodium (mg):**	105.07

Preparation

Blend all ingredients in a blender (add apple juice or rice milk if a thinner consistency is desired).

Raspberry S'Mores

Prep Time: 15 Minutes
Servings: 4

Ingredients

- **8 graham crackers**
- **32 large marshmallows, cut in half**
- **2 1.5-ounce chocolate bars (such as Hershey's™)**
- **1 cup fresh raspberries**

Per Serving

Calories:	372.28	**Omega-3 (g):**	0.09
Protein (g):	4.00	**Omega-6 (g):**	0.75
Carbohydrates (g):	73.90	**Phosphorus (mg):**	72.37
Dietary Fiber (g):	3.17	**Potassium (mg):**	147.41
Fat (g):	8.04	**Sodium (mg):**	147.91

Preparation

Adjust rack to middle position, and heat broiler or toaster oven. Break the crackers in half to form squares, and place on a baking sheet. Arrange 4 marshmallow halves on top of each square. Broil for 30 to 60 seconds or until the marshmallows are golden brown. Break each chocolate bar into 12 pieces. Arrange the chocolate and raspberries on top of half the crackers. Invert the remaining marshmallow-topped crackers onto the raspberry-and-chocolate-topped crackers, pressing gently to make sandwiches. Stack them, if desired.

Ambrosia

Prep Time: 1 Hour 15 Minutes
Servings: 12

Ingredients

- **1 cup sour cream (or light sour cream)**
- **½ cup powdered sugar**
- **½ teaspoon vanilla**
- **1 15-ounce can pineapple chunks, drained**
- **1 15-ounce can sliced peaches, drained**
- **1 ½ cups maraschino cherries, drained**
- **3 cups miniature marshmallows**
- **12 lettuce leaves for serving (optional)**

Per Serving

Calories:	147.63	**Omega-3 (g):**	0.06
Protein (g):	1.23	**Omega-6 (g):**	0.10
Carbohydrates (g):	29.68	**Phosphorus (mg):**	25.20
Dietary Fiber (g):	1.37	**Potassium (mg):**	130.16
Fat (g):	3.47	**Sodium (mg):**	21.18

Preparation

Mix sour cream, powdered sugar and vanilla in a bowl. Add pineapple, peaches, cherries and marshmallows. Gently mix. Let chill in refrigerator for at least 1 hour. If desired, serve on lettuce leaves.

Cherry Cream Pie

Prep Time: 20 Minutes
Servings: 8

Ingredients

- **One 8-ounce package cream cheese, softened**
- **1 cup sugar or Splenda® granular sugar substitute**
- **1 teaspoon vanilla**
- **1 cup nondairy whipped topping or Cool Whip®, thawed**
- **One 9" graham cracker pie crust**
- **One 20-ounce can cherry pie filling, regular or low sugar**

Per Serving

Calories:	451.29	**Omega-3 (g):**	0.23
Protein (g):	3.66	**Omega-6 (g):**	2.19
Carbohydrates (g):	67.14	**Phosphorus (mg):**	59.57
Dietary Fiber (g):	0.87	**Potassium (mg):**	135.72
Fat (g):	19.37	**Sodium (mg):**	272.31

Preparation

In a large bowl, mix cream cheese, sugar or Splenda® and vanilla with a mixer. Add nondairy whipped topping, and mix well. Pour mixture into graham cracker pie crust. Top with cherry pie filling. Refrigerate until ready to serve.

Apple Crisp

Prep Time: 1 Hour
Servings: 8

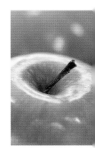

Pr He Pd Tr

Ingredients

Filling
- **7 cups pared, cored and sliced apples**
- **⅓ cup sugar**
- **½ teaspoon nutmeg**
- **½ teaspoon cinnamon**

Topping
- **¾ cup rolled oats**
- **¼ cup brown sugar, packed**
- **2 tablespoons flour**
- **2 tablespoons margarine**

Per Serving

Calories:	152.12	**Omega-3 (g):**	0.09
Protein (g):	0.75	**Omega-6 (g):**	0.85
Carbohydrates (g):	32.14	**Phosphorus (mg):**	20.81
Dietary Fiber (g):	1.59	**Potassium (mg):**	121.04
Fat (g):	3.16	**Sodium (mg):**	49.75

Preparation

Place sliced apples in 9-inch pie pan. Sprinkle sugar and spices over apples. In a small bowl, mix oats, sugar, flour and margarine together until crumbly. Sprinkle over apples. Bake 375° for 35 minutes or until apples are tender and topping is golden brown.

Apricot Tart

Prep Time: 1 Hour
Servings: 6

Pr He Pd Tr

Ingredients

- **1 15-ounce box Pillsbury™ Pie Crusts**
- **⅓ cup slivered almonds**
- **12 Vanilla Wafers**
- **3 tablespoons sugar**
- **8 ripe apricots**
- **1 10-ounce jar apple jelly**
- **1 cup blueberries or blackberries for garnish**

Per Serving

Calories:	413.88	**Omega-3 (g):**	0.19
Protein (g):	4.63	**Omega-6 (g):**	3.49
Carbohydrates (g):	69.72	**Phosphorus (mg):**	73.73
Dietary Fiber (g):	3.58	**Potassium (mg):**	242.75
Fat (g):	14.64	**Sodium (mg):**	203.84

Preparation

Heat oven to 350° F. Fit 1 pie crust into a 9-inch tart pan with a removable bottom (save the other crust for future use). Place the almonds, cookies and sugar in a blender or food processor, and pulse to a fine sand; sprinkle on the bottom of the crust. Halve and pit the apricots. Arrange them, cut-side down, on top of the crumbs. Bake for 25 minutes or until the crust is golden brown. Remove from oven, and cool on a wire rack. Put the jelly into a small saucepan and warm over medium heat until melted and bubbling, stirring constantly. Spoon over the tart. Set aside to cool completely. Garnish with blueberries or blackberries and serve.

Strawberry Cake

Prep Time: 1 Hour
Servings: 12

Ingredients

- **1 package angel food cake mix**
- **One 8-ounce package of light or regular cream cheese, softened**
- **½ cup strawberry preserves or low-sugar strawberry preserves**
- **One 8-ounce container nondairy whipped topping**

Per Serving

Calories:	329.23	**Omega-3 (g):**	0.00
Protein (g):	4.67	**Omega-6 (g):**	0.06
Carbohydrates (g):	48.27	**Phosphorus (mg):**	155.10
Dietary Fiber (g):	0.26	**Potassium (mg):**	109.92
Fat (g):	12.76	**Sodium (mg):**	345.80

Preparation

Bake angel food cake according to package directions. Cool to room temperature. Beat cream cheese and strawberry preserves until smooth. Slice angel food cake into three even horizontal layers. Spread cream cheese mixture between layers, and reassemble. Frost cake, using nondairy whipped topping. Keep refrigerated until ready to serve.

Apricot-Cherry Trifle

Prep Time: 1 Hour
Servings: 6

Ingredients

- **6 ripe apricots, halved and pitted**
- **1 teaspoon fresh lemon juice**
- **2 tablespoons apricot nectar**
- **½ teaspoon vanilla extract**
- **1 angel food cake, cut into ½-inch slices**
- **2 ½ cups nonfat plain yogurt**
- **1 cup bing cherries, halved and pitted**

Per Serving

Calories:	239.93	**Omega-3 (g):**	0.01
Protein (g):	9.96	**Omega-6 (g):**	0.24
Carbohydrates (g):	50.24	**Phosphorus (mg):**	192.00
Dietary Fiber (g):	1.05	**Potassium (mg):**	463.67
Fat (g):	0.08	**Sodium (mg):**	269.00

Not recommended for pre-dialysis patients on a potassium restriction.

Preparation

Cook first 4 ingredients in a medium saucepan over low heat for about 10 minutes or until apricots start to release juices. Remove from heat; set aside. Lay cake slices on waxed paper. Using a standard "rocks" glass, cut out 12 circles of cake. When apricots are cool, puree in blender 2 minutes or until smooth. Cover, and refrigerate 30 minutes. Stir yogurt into apricot mixture. Place a few cherry halves on the bottom of a rocks glass. Spoon 2 tablespoons yogurt-apricot mixture over cherries; cover with a slice of cake; repeat twice. Top with cherries and a drizzle of yogurt-apricot mixture.

Coconut Angel Food Cake

Prep Time: 1 Hour 15 Minutes
Servings: 12

Ingredients

Cake
- **1 ¼ cups egg whites (from about 9 large eggs), at room temperature**
- **¼ teaspoon salt**
- **1 teaspoon cream of tartar**
- **1 cup superfine sugar**
- **2 teaspoons pure vanilla extract**
- **2 teaspoons fresh lemon juice**
- **1 cup sifted cake flour**
- **⅓ cup dry, unsweetened, shredded coconut**
- **⅓ cup fresh coconut shavings**

Sauce
- **1 bag (12 ounces) cranberries, fresh or frozen and thawed**
- **⅔ cup granulated sugar**
- **1 tablespoon grated orange zest**
- **⅔ cup fresh orange juice**
- **2 tablespoons orange-flavored liqueur**
- **½ teaspoon cinnamon**

Per Serving

Calories:	163.32	**Omega-3 (g):**	0.01
Protein (g):	3.90	**Omega-6 (g):**	0.06
Carbohydrates (g):	33.36	**Phosphorus (mg):**	21.43
Dietary Fiber (g):	1.82	**Potassium (mg):**	156.93
Fat (g):	5.25	**Sodium (mg):**	92.17

Preparation

Cake

Preheat oven to 325° F. Beat egg whites and salt in a bowl with an electric mixer on medium until frothy, about 2 minutes. Add cream of tartar. Beat until soft peaks form, about 5 minutes. Increase speed to high. Add ½ cup sugar, 1 tablespoon at a time, until whites form soft, glossy peaks. Beat in vanilla and lemon juice. In another bowl, mix remaining ½ cup sugar with flour. Sift ⅓ sugar-flour mixture over egg whites; gently, but thoroughly, fold into batter using a large spatula. Repeat twice with remaining sugar-flour mixture. Fold in dry coconut in 2 batches. Scrape batter into an ungreased 10-inch angel food tube pan with a removable bottom. Smooth top into even layer. Bake 35 minutes or until top is lightly browned and cake springs back when you press it. Turn pan upside down and rest on the neck of a glass bottle to cool. Run a knife against insides of pan to loosen cake; remove pan. Loosen cake from bottom of pan; invert onto a plate. Cover with plastic wrap. Store at room temperature or in the refrigerator.

Sauce

Boil all ingredients in a medium saucepan 1 minute, until lightly thickened. Let cool. Cover; refrigerate 1 hour. Before serving, sprinkle top of cake with coconut shavings. Serve each slice with 3 tablespoons sauce.

Caramelized Clementines

Prep Time: 1 Hour 15 Minutes
Servings: 6

Ingredients

- **12 clementines, peeled**
- **¼ cup orange liqueur (or dark rum)**
- **1 cup sugar**
- **2 tablespoons lemon juice**
- **⅓ cup water**
- **¼ cup water**
- **¼ cup pomegranate seeds**

Per Serving

Calories:	231.38	Omega-3 (g):	0.00
Protein (g):	1.08	Omega-6 (g):	0.00
Carbohydrates (g):	52.46	Phosphorus (mg):	17.58
Dietary Fiber (g):	1.70	Potassium (mg):	269.14
Fat (g):	.50	Sodium (mg):	1.82

Preparation

Loosen segments of each clementine from the top without detaching from the stem end. Place in a bowl. Sprinkle on liqueur. Cover; refrigerate 30 minutes. To start the sauce, bring ⅓ cup sugar, lemon juice and ⅓ cup water to a boil in a small saucepan over medium heat. Simmer, stirring, until liquid is clear. Remove from heat; set aside. Line baking sheet with foil. To make the shards, stir remaining ⅔ cup sugar and ¼ cup water in a medium saucepan over medium heat until sugar is moistened. Bring to a boil, washing down sides of pan with a brush dipped in cold water, until syrup turns a golden caramel color. Remove from heat. Pour half the caramel onto baking sheet; set aside about 30 minutes to harden. To finish the sauce, add sugar-lemon syrup to remaining caramel in pan. Simmer, stirring often, until caramel dissolves. Transfer to a bowl; cool 15 minutes. Pour over clementines. Cover; refrigerate at least 2 hours. Break hardened caramel into shards; store in an airtight container until ready to serve. Before serving, garnish fruit with caramel shards and pomegranate seeds.

Butternut Squash and Orange Cream

Prep Time: 2 Hours 15 Minutes
Servings: 6

Ingredients

- **1 small butternut squash (about 2 pounds)**
- **1 tablespoon canola oil**
- **6 ounces silken tofu**
- **¼ cup maple syrup (or honey)**
- **½ cup orange juice**
- **½ cup vanilla-flavored soy milk**
- **2 tablespoons grated orange zest**
- **½ cup raspberries (or other seasonal fruit)**
- **⅛ tablespoon grated nutmeg**

Per Serving

Calories:	174.12	Omega-3 (g):	0.22
Protein (g):	4.97	Omega-6 (g):	0.64
Carbohydrates (g):	32.25	Phosphorus (mg):	103.10
Dietary Fiber (g):	4.95	Potassium (mg):	656.47
Fat (g):	4.32	Sodium (mg):	20.86

Not recommended for pre-dialysis patients on a potassium restriction.

Preparation

Preheat oven to 350° F. Brush squash with oil. Bake 1 hour and 20 minutes or until tender. Cool. Cut squash in half, scoop out seeds, and discard. Scoop out 1 cup flesh and transfer to a blender or food processor. Add tofu, syrup, orange juice, soy milk and orange zest, and process until smooth. Spoon equal portions of berries into chilled dessert cups. Pour cream over fruit, and sprinkle nutmeg over top. Chill 30 minutes.

Fruit Sorbet

Prep Time: 20 Minutes
Servings: 8

Pr He Pd Tr

Ingredients

- **One 20-ounce can juice-packed, crushed pineapple, frozen**
- **4 plums, pitted**
- **1 cup frozen raspberries, unsweetened**

Per Serving

Calories:	65.70	**Omega-3 (g):**	0.03
Protein (g):	0.78	**Omega-6 (g):**	0.07
Carbohydrates (g):	16.63	**Phosphorus (mg):**	14.70
Dietary Fiber (g):	2.38	**Potassium (mg):**	162.91
Fat (g):	0.27	**Sodium (mg):**	0.86

Preparation

Thaw pineapple just enough to get out of can and cut into chunks. Place all fruit in food processor and process until pureed. Serve immediately, or spread into an 8-inch by 8-inch pan and freeze.

Grilled Tropical Fruit Shortcake

Prep Time: 1 Hour 30 Minutes
Servings: 4

Pr Pd Tr

Ingredients

- **½ cup water**
- **½ cup granulated sugar**
- **1 teaspoon grated lime peel**
- **2 tablespoons fresh lime juice**
- **1 teaspoon chopped crystallized ginger**
- **PAM® for Grilling Spray**
- **1 firm mango, peeled, pitted and cut into twelve ½-inch thick slices**
- **¼ fresh pineapple, cored, cut crosswise into eight ½-inch pieces**
- **12 large fresh strawberries, tops removed (about 8 ounces)**
- **1 large fresh banana, cut into 8 pieces**
- **4 slices pound cake, 1 inch thick**
- **Whipped light cream**

Per Serving

Calories:	338.91	**Omega-3 (g):**	0.11
Protein (g):	3.45	**Omega-6 (g):**	0.31
Carbohydrates (g):	72.34	**Phosphorus (mg):**	90.78
Dietary Fiber (g):	3.79	**Potassium (mg):**	384.96
Fat (g):	5.52	**Sodium (mg):**	129.21

Not recommended for pre-dialysis patients on a potassium restriction.

Preparation

Combine water, sugar, lime peel, lime juice and ginger in small saucepan. Bring to a boil over high heat. Remove from heat, and cool completely. Reserve ¼ cup syrup and set aside. Spray cold grate of outdoor grill with grilling spray. Prepare grill for medium-low heat. Place mango, pineapple, strawberries and banana in large bowl. Pour remaining syrup over fruit; stir lightly to coat. Thread fruit alternately on 4 metal or heavy wooden skewers. Discard remaining syrup in bowl. Grill kabobs 6 minutes, or until lightly browned, turning once. Brush pound cake slices with some of reserved syrup. Grill 4 minutes, or until lightly browned, turning once. Place each pound cake slice on a dessert plate. Remove fruit from skewers. Top each slice evenly with grilled fruit. Drizzle with remaining reserved syrup. Top each shortcake with a serving of whipped cream. Serve immediately.

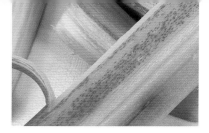

Rhubarb Upside-Down Cake

Prep Time: 1 Hour 40 Minutes
Servings: 10

Ingredients

- **Cooking spray**
- **1 tablespoon dark corn syrup**
- **2 teaspoons butter**
- **½ cup packed light brown sugar**
- **2 tablespoons chopped pecans or walnuts**
- **1 pound rhubarb, trimmed and cut into 1-inch pieces (3 cups)**
- **¾ cup whole-wheat pastry flour**
- **⅓ cup pecans or walnuts**
- **1 teaspoon baking powder**
- **¼ teaspoon salt**
- **2 large egg whites**
- **⅔ cup packed light brown sugar, divided in half**
- **2 large eggs**
- **2 teaspoons freshly grated orange zest**
- **1 teaspoon vanilla extract**

Per Serving

Calories:	185.84	**Omega-3 (g):**	0.03
Protein (g):	3.37	**Omega-6 (g):**	0.52
Carbohydrates (g):	37.25	**Phosphorus (mg):**	83.93
Dietary Fiber (g):	1.17	**Potassium (mg):**	262.79
Fat (g):	2.93	**Sodium (mg):**	158.01

Preparation

Topping

Coat a 10-inch ovenproof skillet (such as cast-iron) with cooking spray. Add corn syrup and butter; heat over low heat until butter has melted, swirling the pan to coat the bottom evenly. Remove from the heat; spread ½ cup brown sugar evenly over the bottom of the pan. Sprinkle chopped nuts over the sugar, and arrange rhubarb, rounded sides down, in a circular pattern on top. Set aside.

Cake

Preheat oven to 375° F. Combine flour, ⅓ cup nuts, baking powder and salt in a food processor or blender; process until finely ground.

Beat 2 egg whites in a large bowl with an electric mixer on high speed until soft peaks form. Gradually add ⅓ cup brown sugar, beating until stiff and glossy. Set aside. (It is not necessary to wash beaters.) Beat whole eggs with the remaining ⅓ cup brown sugar in another large bowl on high speed until thickened and pale, 3 to 5 minutes. Blend in orange zest and vanilla.

Whisk one-fourth of the beaten whites into the whole-egg mixture. Gently fold in half the flour mixture. Fold in the remaining beaten whites, followed by the remaining flour mixture. Spread the batter evenly over the rhubarb.

Bake the cake until the top springs back when touched lightly, 25 to 30 minutes. Let cool in the pan on a wire rack for 5 minutes. Loosen the edges with a knife. Invert a serving platter over the cake. Using oven mitts, grasp platter and skillet together, and carefully flip them over. Let the skillet sit for a few minutes to allow any caramel clinging to it to drip onto the cake. Remove the skillet. Let the cake cool for at least 20 minutes. Serve warm or at room temperature.

Strawberry Lime Dessert

Prep Time: 45 Minutes

Servings: 6

| Pr | He | Pd | Tr |

Ingredients

- **4 cups fresh strawberries, stems removed, and quartered (about 3 cups quartered berries)**
- **½ cup whipping cream**
- **1 tablespoon sugar**
- **¼ teaspoon finely shredded lime peel**
- **1 lime, cut into 6 to 8 wedges**

Per Serving

Calories:	56.79	**Omega-3 (g):**	0.08
Protein (g):	0.92	**Omega-6 (g):**	0.12
Carbohydrates (g):	11.70	**Phosphorus (mg):**	30.79
Dietary Fiber (g):	2.35	**Potassium (mg):**	173.96
Fat (g):	1.44	**Sodium (mg):**	7.74

Preparation

In a shallow dish, mash 1 cup of the quartered strawberries with a potato masher. (Or puree with a mini food chopper, food processor or blender.) In a medium bowl, beat whipping cream, sugar and lime peel until cream is very stiff. Fold in mashed strawberries. In individual 6- to 7-ounce glasses or dishes, layer whipped cream mixture and remaining strawberries. Top each serving with a fresh lime wedge. Serve immediately, or cover and chill up to 2 hours before serving.

Blackberry Cobbler

Prep Time: 1 Hour

Servings: 6

| Pr | Pd | Tr |

Ingredients

- **Butter for the baking dish**
- **3 half-pint containers fresh blackberries or one 16-ounce bag**
- **Frozen unsweetened blackberries, thawed**
- **3 tablespoons confectioner's sugar**
- **2 cups pancake mix**
- **1 cup whole milk**
- **2 large eggs**
- **1 7- or 8-ounce container whipped cream**

Per Serving

Calories:	463.82	**Omega-3 (g):**	0.41
Protein (g):	11.35	**Omega-6 (g):**	1.45
Carbohydrates (g):	53.55	**Phosphorus (mg):**	427.40
Dietary Fiber (g):	4.99	**Potassium (mg):**	463.05
Fat (g):	23.31	**Sodium (mg):**	671.28

Not recommended for pre-dialysis patients on a potassium restriction.

Preparation

Heat oven to 375° F. Butter an 8-inch square baking dish. Add the berries and 1 ½ tablespoons of the sugar to the dish, and toss. In a large bowl, combine the pancake mix, milk and eggs until no lumps remain. Pour the batter over the berries. Bake until the crust is golden and a toothpick inserted in the center comes out clean, about 30 minutes. Remove from oven. Let cool for 5 minutes. Sprinkle with the remaining sugar, and serve with a dollop of whipped cream.

Key Lime Pie

Prep Time: 1 Hour 15 Minutes
Servings: 10

Pr **Tr**

Ingredients

Crust (or use a commercially prepared graham crust such as Keebler® Ready Crust Graham Cracker Pie Crust)

- **1 ½ cups graham crackers, crushed**
- **¼ cup sugar**
- **5 tablespoons butter, melted**

Filling

- **1 can (14 ounces) nonfat, sweetened, condensed milk**
- **½ cup fresh lime juice**
- **1 tablespoon lime zest, minced**
- **1 egg**
- **2 eggs, yolks and whites separated**
- **¼ teaspoon cream of tartar**
- **2 cups low-calorie whipped cream (such as Cool Whip®)**
- **1 lime, thinly sliced (optional)**

Per Serving

Calories:	348.65	**Omega-3 (g):**	0.13
Protein (g):	6.59	**Omega-6 (g):**	0.99
Carbohydrates (g):	38.98	**Phosphorus (mg):**	161.52
Dietary Fiber (g):	0.65	**Potassium (mg):**	244.00
Fat (g):	19.42	**Sodium (mg):**	197.15

Preparation

Preheat oven to 325° F. For crust: Mix graham cracker crumbs with sugar and butter. Spread evenly over bottom and sides of a nonstick 9" pie pan, and bake 5 minutes. Remove from oven; let cool. For filling: In a medium bowl, using a fork, beat milk, lime juice and zest. Add 1 whole egg and 2 egg yolks (reserve whites), and beat well. Set aside. In a large mixing bowl, beat egg whites until foamy. After about 20 seconds, add cream of tartar. Fold whites into custard mixture, and pour into partially baked crust. Bake 45 to 60 minutes or until set. Let cool. Serve with whipped cream. Garnish with lime slices.

Mango Gratin

Prep Time: 25 Minutes
Servings: 2

Pr **Pe** **Tr**

Ingredients

- **1 large ripe mango**
- **Grated zest and juice of 1 lime**
- **½ cup vanilla yogurt**
- **2 tablespoons brown sugar**
- **2 teaspoons butter**

Per Serving

Calories:	177.73	**Omega-3 (g):**	0.07
Protein (g):	2.79	**Omega-6 (g):**	0.79
Carbohydrates (g):	30.97	**Phosphorus (mg):**	75.47
Dietary Fiber (g):	2.05	**Potassium (mg):**	312.5
Fat (g):	6.13	**Sodium (mg):**	61.46

Preparation

Heat broiler. Using a heavy, sharp knife, slice the mango lengthwise around each side of the pit. Remove the skin, and cut the fruit into bite-sized pieces. Divide between 2 small ramekins, and stir in the lime zest. Top with the yogurt and brown sugar, and dot with the butter. Spritz with the lime juice. Broil 2 to 3 minutes or just until the topping melts and browns.

Index

Refrigeration Chart

Food	Refrigerate	Freeze
Beef steaks	1 to 2 days	6 to 12 months
Beef roasts	1 to 2 days	6 to 12 months
Corned beef	7 days	2 weeks
Pork chops	1 to 2 days	3 to 4 months
Pork roasts	1 to 2 days	4 to 8 months
Fresh sausage	1 to 2 days	1 to 2 months
Smoked sausage	7 days	Not recommended
Cured ham	5 to 7 days	1 to 2 months
Canned ham	1 year	Not recommended
Ham slice	3 days	1 to 2 months
Bacon	7 days	2 to 4 months
Veal cutlets	1 to 2 days	6 to 9 months
Stew meat	1 to 2 days	3 to 4 months
Ground meat	1 to 2 days	3 to 4 months
Luncheon meats	3 to 5 days	Not recommended
Frankfurters	7 days	1 month
Whole chicken	1 to 2 days	12 months
Chicken pieces	1 to 2 days	9 months

Freezing Tips

• List the date on all items before placing them in the freezer.

• Freezing canned hams or processed meats is not recommended. Frozen canned hams become watery and soft when thawed. Processed meats have a high salt content, which speeds rancidity when thawed.

• Do not freeze stuffed chickens or turkeys. The stuffing may incur bacterial contamination during the lengthy thawing process.

• Partially thawed food that still has ice crystals in the package can be safely refrozen. A safer test is to determine if the surface temperature is 40 degrees Fahrenheit or lower.

Baking Equivalents

When the recipe calls for	Use
Baking	
½ cup (1 stick) butter	4 ounces
2 cups (4 sticks) butter	1 pound
4 cups all-purpose flour	1 pound
4½ cups sifted cake flour	1 pound
1 square chocolate	1 ounce
1 cup semisweet chocolate chips	6 ounces
4 cups marshmallows	1 pound
2¼ cups packed brown sugar	1 pound
4 cups confectioners' sugar	1 pound
2 cups sugar	1 pound
Cereal/Bread	
1 cup fine dry bread crumbs	4 to 5 slices
1 cup soft bread crumbs	2 slices
1 cup small bread crumbs	2 slices
1 cup fine saltine crumbs	28 saltines
1 cup fine graham cracker crumbs	15 graham crackers
1 cup vanilla wafer crumbs	22 wafers
1 cup crushed cornflakes	3 cups uncrushed
4 cups cooked macaroni	8 ounces uncooked
3½ cups cooked rice	1 cup uncooked
Dairy	
1 cup shredded cheese	4 ounces
1 cup cottage cheese	8 ounces
1 cup sour cream	8 ounces
1 cup whipped cream	½ cup heavy cream
⅔ cup evaporated milk	1 (5⅓-ounce) can
1⅔ cups evaporated milk	1 (13-ounce) can
Fruit	
4 cups sliced or chopped apples	4 medium
1 cup mashed bananas	3 medium
2 cups pitted cherries	4 cups unpitted
2½ cups shredded coconut	8 ounces
4 cups cranberries	1 pound
1 cup pitted dates	1 (8-ounce) package
1 cup candied fruit	1 (8-ounce) package
3 to 4 tablespoons lemon juice plus 1 tablespoon grated lemon peel	1 lemon
⅓ cup orange juice plus 2 teaspoons grated orange peel	1 orange
4 cups sliced peaches	8 medium
2 cups pitted prunes	1 (12-ounce) package
3 cups raisins	1 (15-ounce) package

Garnishes

Bell Pepper Garnishes: Accent rice dishes with sautéed julienned red, yellow, and green bell peppers.

Butter Curls: Dip the blade of a vegetable peeler into hot water and pull firmly over a slightly softened stick of butter. Chill the curls in ice water.

Carrot Curls: Scrape fresh carrots to remove the tough outer skin. Use a potato peeler to make thin strips down the length of the carrot. Roll up the strips, secure with wooden picks, and chill in ice water until crisp and curled.

Celery Curls: Cut celery ribs into short pieces. Slice the ends lengthwise; both ends may be cut if desired. Chill the cut celery in ice water until the cut ends curl.

Chocolate Curls: Pour melted chocolate onto a baking sheet lined with waxed paper. Spread the chocolate in a 2- to 3-inch strip. Let stand until the chocolate is cooled and slightly sticky but not firm. Pull a vegetable peeler slowly across the chocolate until a curl forms, allowing the chocolate to curl on top of the peeler. Use a wooden pick to transfer the curl to a plate. Chill until needed.

Cooked Vegetable Garnishes: Decorate large platters with bundles of julienned carrots and celery tied with chives, slices of baked sweet potato, or thin wedges of baked acorn squash.

Cookie Trimmers: Coat rolls of chilled cookie dough with minced candied fruit, chopped nuts, or candy sprinkles before slicing and baking.

Fluted Fruit Wheels: Cut thin strips of peel evenly from the stem end to blossom ends of lemons, oranges, and limes. Cut the fruit into slices of the desired thickness. To make twists, cut from one side to the center and twist. For fans, slice fruit to but not through the bottom side; fan out the slices.

Fluted Mushroom: Select firm, round white mushrooms. Rub gently with lemon juice to prevent discoloration. Press the flat tip of a knife into the center of the mushroom cap in a star design. Continue making indentations in rows around the mushroom cap.

Frosted Fruit: Rinse and dry grapes, cranberries, or cherries. Dip in egg whites beaten until frothy, then in granulated sugar; shake off excess sugar and let dry.

Grape Ice Cubes: Make ice cubes for party beverages using white grape juice and freeze a green grape in each.

Green Onion Frills: Cut off the root end and most of the stem portion of green onions. Make narrow lengthwise cuts at both ends with a sharp knife to produce a fringe. Chill in ice water until the ends curl.

Herb Bundles: Decorate meat platters with bundles of herbs used in preparing the dish, such as watercress, parsley, thyme, rosemary, or sage.

Kumquat Flower: Cut a canned kumquat into six wedges to but not through the bottom to make petals.

Radish Accordion: Select long, narrow radishes. Cut a thin slice from each end. Slice crosswise to but not through the bottom side. Chill in ice water until the slices open.

Radish Mum: Select round radishes. Trim off the root ends. Make several thin crosswise cuts almost to the bottom of the radish. Make additional cuts perpendicular to the first cuts. Chill in ice water until the radish opens.

Radish Rose: Select round radishes. Cut a thin slice from each end. Cut 4 or 5 thin petal-shape slices around the outer edge from top to bottom, leaving the bottom intact. Chill in ice water until the petals open.

Strawberry Fans: Select large firm strawberries with caps. Cut several parallel slices from the tip of each berry to just below the cap with a sharp knife. Spead the slices gently to form a fan.

Tomato Rose: Cut the peel gently from a firm tomato in a continuous ¼-inch strip with a sharp knife. Shape the peel into a rose, starting at the base end and placing the skin side out. Add fresh herb leaves such as basil to resemble rose leaves.

Herbs

Use fresh whole herbs when possible. When fresh herbs are not available, use dried whole herbs that can be crushed just while adding. Store herbs in airtight containers away from the heat of the stove. Fresh herbs may be layered between paper towels and microwaved on High for 2 minutes or until dry.

Basil .... Can be chopped and added to cold poultry salads. If the recipe calls for tomatoes or tomato sauce, add a touch of basil to bring out a rich flavor.

Bay leaf .... The basis of many French seasonings. It is added to soups, stews, marinades, and stuffings.

Bouquet garni .... A bundle of parsley, thyme, and bay leaves tied together and added to stews, soups, or sauces. Other herbs and spices may be added to the basic herbs.

Chervil .... One of the traditional fines herbes used in French cooking. (The others are tarragon, parsley, and chives.) It is good in omelets and soups.

Chives .... Available fresh, dried, or frozen, chives can be substituted for fresh onion or shallot in nearly any recipe.

Garlic .... One of the oldest herbs in the world, it must be carefully handled. For best results, press or crush the garlic clove.

Marjoram .... An aromatic herb of the mint family, it is good in soups, sauces, stuffings, and stews.

Mint .... Use fresh, dried, or ground with vegetables, desserts, fruits, jelly, lamb, or tea. Fresh sprigs of mint make attractive aromatic garnishes.

Oregano .... A staple, savory herb in Italian, Spanish, Greek, and Mexican cuisines. It is very good in dishes with a tomato foundation, especially in combination with basil.

Parsley .... Use this mild herb as fresh sprigs or dried flakes to flavor or garnish almost any dish.

Rosemary .... This pungent herb is especially good in poultry and fish dishes and in such accompaniments as stuffings.

Saffron .... Use this deep-orange herb, made from the dried stamens of a crocus, sparingly in poultry, seafood, and rice dishes.

Sage .... This herb is a perennial favorite with all kinds of poultry and stuffings.

Tarragon .... One of the fines herbes. Goes well with all poultry dishes whether hot or cold.

Thyme .... A widely used herb, thyme is usually used in combination with bay leaf in soups, stews, and sauces.

Notes

Order Information

Thank you for your purchase of *Brilliant Eats: Simple and Delicious Recipes for Anyone Who Wants to Be KidneyWise™*. All proceeds from book sales will benefit the PKD Foundation, the only organization, worldwide, dedicated to finding a treatment and cure for polycystic kidney disease (PKD).

To order additional copies of

Brilliant Eats
Simple and Delicious Recipes for Anyone Who Wants to Be KidneyWise™

visit **www.kidneywise.org** or call **1-800-PKD CURE**.

Brilliant Eats: Simple and Delicious Recipes for Anyone Who Wants to Be KidneyWise™ is one component of the KidneyWise™ Nutrition Program. To learn more, visit **www.kidneywise.org**.